Frederick Morgan Padelford

Old English Musical Terms

Frederick Morgan Padelford

Old English Musical Terms

ISBN/EAN: 9783337087234

Printed in Europe, USA, Canada, Australia, Japan

Cover: Foto ©Thomas Meinert / pixelio.de

More available books at **www.hansebooks.com**

BONNER BEITRÄGE ZUR ANGLISTIK
HERAUSGEGEBEN VON PROF. DR. M. TRAUTMANN.

HEFT IV.

OLD ENGLISH MUSICAL TERMS

BY

FREDERICK MORGAN PADELFORD
FELLOW IN ENGLISH OF YALE UNIVERSITY

BONN 1899
P. HANSTEIN'S VERLAG

TO

PROFESSOR ALBERT S. COOK

WHO INSPIRES IN HIS STUDENTS THE IDEAL
OF A HARMONIOUS LIFE

THIS STUDY IS DEDICATED

V

Preface.

The aim of this study is twofold: to contribute something to the exhaustive knowledge of Old English words, and to further our appreciation of the æsthetic character of the pre-Norman civilization. I have endeavored to accomplish this twofold result by making a complete glossary of Old English musical terms, and by supplementing this glossary with an introductory essay. That the glossary is complete, and, still more, that no significant references have been omitted, I hardly dare to hope. Yet I feel confident that the work is not without value, for the only extant consideration of the subject is in a monograph by Wackerbarth, which is both meagre and incorrect.

The scheme of the glossary is as follows: when the musical character of a word admits of some doubt, the word is preceded by a mark of interrogation; if the musical character is very doubtful, the word is inclosed in brackets. A few words have been admitted on the authority of other glossarists, as *beorhtm* and *dreamswinsung*; these, however, I have indicated as being very doubtful. Generally, only the musical definitions of a word of several meanings are given; if, however, some of the meanings shade into the musical, these are included in brackets. If the definition of a word is questionable, it is followed by a mark of interrogation. Words which signify the canonical hours, being musical only indirectly, are referred to an exhaustive article in the Publications of the Modern

Language Association. When the Latin equivalent of a word is known, it is indicated either in the references to the glosses, which are placed first among the references, or in the collection of Scriptural and hymnic translations, or it is printed after the definition; in case several Latin equivalents are printed after the definition, they are followed directly by index letters, and these letters are again placed before those references from the Old English texts which translate the corresponding Latin words. A classification of the references is made, when possible, and this classification is designed to throw light upon the problems which attend the use of the word. When a mark of interrogation precedes a reference, some doubt as to the applicability of the reference is expressed.

This monograph was written at the suggestion of Professor Albert S. Cook, and under his supervision, and the counsel and inspiration received from him have been invaluable. I wish to acknowledge my indebtedness to Dr. Caroline L. White, who gave many timely suggestions, to Dr. Bertha E. Lovewell, who furnished me with the advance sheets of the Saints' Lives, which she had received through the kindness of Professor Skeat, and to the Library of Harvard University for the use of books.

Contents.

	page
Table of Abbreviations	VIII
Introduction	1
Glossary	63
Appendixes:	
I. Latin and Old English Equivalents	108
II. Modern English and Old English Equivalents	110

Table of Abbreviations.

Æ. Coll. = Ælfrici Colloquium in W. W. Quoted by page and line.
Æ. Gl. = Ælfric's Grammatik und Glossar, J. Zupitza, Berlin, 1880. Quoted by page and line.
Æ. Gr. = See preceding paragraph.
Æ. H. = The Homilies of Ælfric, B. Thorpe for the Ælfric Society, London, 1844—46. Quoted by volume, page and line.
Æ. LS. = Ælfric's Lives of the Saints, W. W. Skeat, EETS., Nos. 76, 82, (in preparation) 1881, 1890, (—). Quoted by number and line.
Æ. PE. = Ælfric's Pastoral Epistle in AL. Quoted by section.
AL. = Ancient Laws and Institutes of England, B. Thorpe, Public Records, 1840.
An. = Andreas, Bibl. P., vol. 2.
Angl. = Anglia, Zeitschrift für Englische Philologie, Halle, 1878—.
Apstls. = Die Schicksale der Apostel, Bibl. P., vol. 2.
ASH. = Anglo-Saxon Hymnarium, J. Stevenson for Surtees Society, vol. 23. Quoted by page and line.
B. T. = An Anglo-Saxon Dictionary, Based on the Manuscript Collections of J. Bosworth, T. N. Toller, Oxford, 1882—1898.
B. = Beowulf, Bibl. P., vol. 1.
Bd. = The Old English Version of Bede's Ecclesiastical History of the English People, T. Miller, EETS., Nos. 95, 96, 1890—1891. Quoted by page and line.
BH. = Blickling Homilies, R. Morris, EETS., Nos. 58, 63, 1874—1876. Quoted by page and line.
Bibl. P. = Bibliothek der Angelsächsischen Poesie, C. W. M. Grein, R. P. Wülker. 1. Band, Kassel, 1883; 2. Band, Kassel, 1888; 3. Band, Leipzig, 1897. Quoted by line.
Bibl. Pr. = Bibliothek der Angelsächsischen Prosa, C. W. M. Grein, R. P. Wülker. 1. Band, Kassel-Göttingen, 1872; 2. Band, Kassel, 1885; 3. Band, Kassel, 1889. Quoted by line unless otherwise specified.
Blick. Gl. = Glosses taken from a copy of the Roman Psalter in the Library at Blickling Hall. Printed at the end of the Blickling Homilies. See BH.

Table of Abbreviations. IX

- BR. = The Rule of S. Benet, Latin and Anglo-Saxon Interlinear Version, H. Logeman, EETS., No. 90, 1888. Quoted by page and line.
- Bt. = King Alfred's Anglo-Saxon Version of Boethius' De Consolatione Philosophiæ, Samuel Fox, London, 1864. Quoted by page and line.
- Byrht. = Byrhtferth's Handboc, Kluge, Anglia, vol. S. Quoted by line.
- By. = Byrhtnoth's Tod, Bibl. P., vol. 1.
- C. Æ. = The Canons of Ælfric in AL. Quoted by section.
- Cart. Sax. = Cartularium Saxonicum, a Collection of Charters relating to Anglo-Saxon History, W. de Gray Birch, London 1883—1893. Quoted by volume page and line.
- CD. = Codex Diplomaticus Aevi Saxonici, J. Kemble, Publications of the English Historical Society, 1839—1848. Quoted by volume and page.
- C. Edg. = Canons enacted under King Edgar, in AL. Quoted by section.
- Chad = Leben des Chad, A. Napier, Anglia, vol. 10. Quoted by line.
- Chart. Th. = Diplomatarium Anglicum Aevi Saxonici, B. Thorpe, London, 1865. Quoted by page and line.
- Chr. = Cynewulf's Christ, Bibl. P., vol. 3.
- Corpus Gl. = Corpus Glosses, H. Sweet in The Oldest English Texts, EETS., No. 83, 1885. Quoted by number.
- C. Ps. = Eadwine's Canterbury Psalter, F. Harsley, EETS., No. 92, 1889. Quoted by psalm and verse.
- Dan. = Daniel, Bibl. P., vol. 2.
- DCM. = De Consuetudine Monachorum, W. S. Logeman, Anglia, vol. 13. Quoted by line.
- Deor. = Des Sängers Trost, Bibl. P., vol. 1.
- Deut. = Deuteronomium, Bibl. Pr., vol. 1.
- Dip. Ang. = Diplomatarium Anglicum Ævi Saxonici, B. Thorpe, London, 1865. Quoted by page and line.
- DJ. = Das Jüngste Gericht, Bibl. P., vol. 3.
- Dox. = Paraphrasis Poetica in Doxologiam, J. R. Lumby, EETS., No. 65, 1876. Quoted by line.
- Eccl. Inst. = Ecclesiastical Institutes in AL. Quoted by page.
- El. = Elene, Bibl. P., vol. 2.
- Emb. = Botschaft des Gemahls, Bibl. P., vol. 1.
- Ep. Alex. = Epistola Alexandri, W. M. Baskervill, Anglia, vol. 4. Quoted by line.
- Epinal Gl. = Epinal Glossary, H. Sweet in The Oldest English Texts, EETS., No. 83, 1885. Quoted by number.
- Ex. = Exodus, Bibl. Pr., vol. 1.
- Exod. = Exodus, Bibl. P., vol. 2.
- Fates of Men = Der Menschen Geschicke, Bibl. P., vol. 3.
- Fin. = Der Kampf um Finnsburg, Bibl. P., vol. 1.

Table of Abbreviations.

Gen. = Genesis, Bibl. P., vol. 2.
Genesis = Genesis, Bibl. Pr., vol. 1.
Gifts of Men = Der Menschen Gaben, Bibl. P., vol. 3.
Gn. V. = Versus Gnomici, Gr. Bibl. P.
G. P. C. = The Anglo-Saxon Version of Gregory's Pastoral Care, H. Sweet, EETS., Nos. 45, 50, 1871—1872. Quoted by page and line.
Gr. Bibl. P. = Bibliothek der Angelsächsischen Poesie, C. W. M. Grein, 2. Band, Göttingen, 1858. Quoted by line unless otherwise specified.
Gr. BR. = Die Angelsächsischen Prosabearbeitungen der Benedictinerregel, A. Schröer, Bibl. Pr., vol. 2. Quoted by page and line.
Gr. Dial. = The Anglo-Saxon Version of Gregory's Dialogues. Quoted from Lye. See Wanley's Catalogue, p. 71.
Gr. Pr. 3. = Angelsächsische Homilien und Heiligenleben, B. Assman, Bibl. Pr., vol. 3.
Gu. = Guthlac, Bibl. P., vol. 3.
Hall = Concise Anglo-Saxon Dictionary, J. R. C. Hall, London, 1894.
Harr. H. = Höllenfahrt Christi, Bibl. P., vol. 3.
Herr. Arch. = Ein weiteres Bruchstück der Regularis Concordia, J. Zupitza, vol. 84 of Archiv für das Studium der Neueren Sprachen, Braunschweig, 1846—. Quoted by line.
Hpt. Gl. = Angelsächsische Glossen, vol. 9 of Zeitschrift für Deutsches Alterthum, M. Haupt, Leipzig. Quoted by page and original line number.
Hy. = Hymnen und Gebete, C. W. M. Grein, Bibliothek der Angelsächsischen Poesie, 2. Band, Göttingen, 1858.
Josh. = Josue, Bibl. Pr., vol. 1.
Judg. = Liber Judicum, Bibl. Pr., vol. 1.
Judith = Judith, Bibl. P., vol. 2.
Jul. = Juliana, Bibl. P., vol. 3.
Klgk. = Altenglische Kleinigkeiten, A. Napier, Anglia, vol. 11. Quoted by section and line.
Lamb. Ps. = An Interlinear Version of the Psalms in a Ms. preserved in the Library of Lambeth Place. Quoted by psalm and verse.
Lchdm. = Leechdoms, Wortcunning, and Starcraft of Early England, O. Cockayne, London, 1864—1866. Quoted by volume, page and line.
Leiden Gl. = Leiden Glossary, H. Sweet in The Oldest English Texts, EETS., No. 83, 1885. Quoted by number.
Leo = Angelsächsisches Glossar, H. Leo, Halle, 1877.
L. Eth. = Laws of King Ethelred, in AL. Quoted by section.
Lind. John = The Lindisfarne John, in The Gospel according to St. John in Anglo-Saxon and Northumbrian Versions

Table of Abbreviations. XI

	synoptically arranged, W. W. Skeat, Cambridge, 1878. Quoted by chapter and verse.
Lind. Lk. =	The Lindisfarne Luke, in The Gospel according to St. Luke in Anglo-Saxon and Northumbrian Versions synoptically arranged, W. W. Skeat, Cambridge, 1874. Quoted by chapter and verse.
Lind. Mk. =	The Lindisfarne Mark, in The Gospel according to St. Mark in Anglo-Saxon and Northumbrian Versions synoptically arranged, W. W. Skeat, Cambridge, 1871. Quoted by chapter and verse.
Lind. Mt. =	The Lindisfarne Matthew, in The Gospel according to St. Matthew in Anglo-Saxon and Northumbrian Versions synoptically arranged, W. W. Skeat, Cambridge, 1887. Quoted by chapter and verse.
L. Ine =	The Laws of King Ine, in AL. Quoted by section.
Lords Pr. =	Paraphrasis Poetica in Orationem Dominicam, J. R. Lumby, EETS., No. 65, 1876. Quoted by line.
Lorica Prayer =	Oldest English Texts, p. 174. See V. Ps.
LR. =	Ranks, in AL. Quoted by section.
L. Wiht. =	The Laws of King Wihtræd, in AL. Quoted by section.
Men. =	Heiligenkalendar, Bibl. P., vol. 2.
Met. =	The Anglo-Saxon Metrical Version of the Metrical Portions of Boethius, Gr. Bibl. P. Quoted by number of metre and line.
Mon. P. =	Be Manna Mode, Gr. Bibl. P.
Napier Gl. =	Altenglische Glossen, A. Napier, vol. 11 of Englische Studien, Organ für Englische Philologie, Leipzig, 1877—. Quoted by page.
New Ald. Gl. =	New Aldhelm Glosses, H. Logeman, Anglia, vol. 13. Quoted by number.
ONT. =	Ælfric de Vetere et Novo Testamento, Bibl. Pr., vol. 1. Quoted by page and line.
Or. =	King Alfred's Orosius, H. Sweet, EETS., No. 79, 1883. Quoted by page and line.
Pa. =	Panther, Bibl. P., vol. 3.
Ph. =	Phoenix, Bibl. P., vol. 3.
PMLA. =	Anglo-Saxon Dægmæl, Frederick Tupper, Publications of the Modern Language Association, Baltimore, 1895.
Prud. Gl. =	Die Bouloneser Angelsächsischen Glossen zu Prudentius, A. Holder, Germania, vol. 11 (new series). Quoted by page and number.
R. =	Rätsel, Bibl. P., vol. 3.
Rim. P. =	Reimlied, Bibl. P., vol. 3.
Rood =	Traumgesicht vom Kreuze Christi, Bibl. P., vol. 2.
Rush. John =	The Rushworth John. See Lind. John.
Rush. Lk. =	The Rushworth Luke. See Lind. Lk.
Rush. Mk. =	The Rushworth Mark. See Lind. Mk.
Rush. Mt. =	The Rushworth Matthew. See Lind. Mt.

Sal. = Anglo-Saxon Dialogues of Salomon and Saturn, J.M. Kemble for the Ælfric Society, London, 1845—1848. Quoted by line.
Sat. = Christ und Satan, Bibl. P., vol. 2, pp. 521—562.
SC. = Two Saxon Chronicles, Earle and Plummer, Oxford, 1892.
Schmid = Die Gesetze der Angelsachsen, R. Schmid, Leipzig, 1858.
Scop = Des Sängers Weitfahrt, Bibl. P., vol. 1.
Seaf. = Seefahrer, Bibl. P., vol. 1.
Shrn. = The Shrine. A Collection of Occasional Papers on Dry Subjects, O. Cockayne, London, 1864—1870. Quoted by page and line.
Skt. John = The Corpus Christi John. See Lind. John.
Skt. Lk. = The Corpus Christi Luke. See Lind. Lk.
Skt. Mk. = The Corpus Christi Mark. See Lind. Mk.
Skt. Mt. = The Corpus Christi Matthew. See Lind. Mt.
Smith's Bd. = Baedae Historia Ecclesiastica, J. Smith, Cantabrigiae, 1722. Quoted by page and line.
Som. = Dictionarium Saxonico-Latino-Anglicum, E. Somner, Oxford, 1659.
Soul's Ad. = Rede der Seele an den Leichnam, Bibl. P., vol. 2.
Spl. Ps. = Psalterium Davidis Latino-Saxonicum Vetus, J. Spelman, London, 1640. Quoted by psalm and verse.
St. Gu. = The Anglo-Saxon Version of the Life of St. Guthlac, C. W. Goodwin, London, 1848. Quoted by page and line.
Techmer = Internationale Zeitschrift für Allgemeine Sprachwissenschaft, F. Techmer, Leipzig, 1891—94. Quoted by volume, page, and line.
Th. Ps = Libri Psalmorum Versio Antiqua Latina, B. Thorpe, Oxford, 1835. Quoted by psalm and verse.
V. Ps. = Vespasian Psalter, H. Sweet, Oldest English Texts, EETS., No. 83, 1885. Quoted by psalm and verse.
Vesp. H. = Vespasian Hymns. See V. Ps. Quoted by hymn and line.
Wand. = Wanderer, Bibl. P., vol. 1.
Wanl. Cat. = Wanley's Catalogue of Anglo-Saxon MSS., forming the third volume of Hickes' Thesaurus, Oxford, 1705.
W. H. = Wulfstan: Sammlung der ihm zugeschriebenen Homilien, nebst Untersuchung über ihre Echtheit, A. Napier, Berlin, 1883. Quoted by page and line.
Whale = Der Walfisch, Bibl. P., vol. 3.
Wond. Cre. = Wunder der Schöpfung, Bibl. P., vol. 3.
W. W. = Anglo-Saxon and Old English Vocabularies, T. Wright; second edition by R. P. Wülker, London, 1884. Quoted by column and line.
Zu. Ap. = The Anglo-Saxon Version of the Story of Apollonius of Type, J. Zupitza, vol. 97 of Archiv für das Studium der Neueren Sprachen, Braunschweig, 1846—. Quoted by page and line.

Introduction.

Music before the Migration.

The Old English were a music-loving people. Music was as natural to them as the intense and passionate character which made it inevitable. If, perchance, we read the fragments of the first epic songs, originated in the dim light of the centuries preceding the migration, and suggesting a long development from harmonious antecedents; or if we read the last homily or saint's life; we find the same consistent affection for song.

Glowing is the picture of that Widsith, the far-traveled minstrel, who leaves the hall of his dear lord, and wanders north and south with his lays of heroes and battles. 'Widsith spake, his word-hoard unlocked, he who most of men had journeyed 'mongst the tribes and folk of the earth; oft he in hall had received pleasant gifts, he of the Myrgings sprung. He with Ealhhild, the faithful peace-weaver, for the first time had sought the home of the Hreth-king, eastward of Anglia, Eormanric, fierce breaker of treaties. Began he of many things to speak: "I have learned that many men rule over tribes; each prince should govern his life by right conduct, one earl after the other should care for his realm, he who wishes his throne to prosper."[1]

Then this visitor of Attila and Gunther describes the courts he has visited, the battles he has seen, as he traversed the spacious earth. A long time he tarried with Eormanric, who gave him a precious ring, and, when he returned home, he gave this to his liege lord, who had bestowed an estate upon

---
[1] Widsið 1 ff.

him. But Ealhhild the queen, seeing his magnanimity, gave the minstrel another ring, and in gratitude he spread in song her fame over many lands.

Scilling is his companion, and together they gladden the hearts of warriors: 'Then I and Scilling with clear voice before our victorious lord uplifted the song; loud to the harp the melody sounded. Then many men, haughty of soul, declared that well they knew a better lay they had never heard'.[1] They wander over the earth, favored of men: 'So wandering as fate decrees, over the lands of many men the gleemen go, their needs express, and thanks return. Ever north or south some one they meet, loving song and generous in gifts, who will achieve his fame amidst his nobles, show his courage, till all things vanish,—even light and life. Such an one merits praise, hath under heaven lasting honor.'[2]

This song of Widsith gives a clear idea of the court minstrel of the early Germans. He was beloved by his lord, honored with lands, and the delight of every feast. His lays told of bravery and beauty, as Widsith sang of the courage of Wudga and Hama in the battles of the Huns and Goths, and of the queenliness of Ealhhild. His instrument was the harp, which held favor with the Germanic peoples for centuries.

The clear-voiced song of the minstrel and the melody of the harp scarcely die away in the Beowulf, but throughout the saga the music is heard as an undertone. The joyous music of Heorot was heard by Grendel day after day, the minstrels lay carried the deeds of the monster to the courts of the earth, and thus the crime came to the ears of Beowulf. There was music after Beowulf's arrival when the ale was passed about the hall; again the music sounded when Beowulf had made his vow. An old bard, proud of his power, chanted the adventures of Beowulf when his triumph over Grendel was known; again and again the hall rang with music when the feast of rejoicing was held. When Beowulf returned to his home, he described vividly to Hygelac the music of Heorot: 'There was song and glee; the venerable Scylding, versed in many things, told tales of far-off times. Now one brave in war awoke the joy of the harp, touched the gleewood; now a

---

[1] ibid. 103 ff.   [2] ibid. 135 ff.

true and grievous lay was chanted; now the large-hearted king with care unfolded a wondrous story; and now one bound by the fetters of age, a hoary warrior, would regret youth with its battle-strength, as he, wise with the lapse of winters, recalled many things.'[1]

The saga was not the exclusive possession of any class, for here are heard, beside the minstrel, the warrior the old sage, and the king. Indeed, the Beowulf bears interesting testimony to the conclusion that the sagas were in part the production and property of the community, in part the work of the individual. For no sooner had Beowulf overcome Grendel than one versed in song began to compose cunningly the adventures of Beowulf, to couple them with Sigemund's, and to contrast them with Heremod's, thus beginning to shape, in the rough, the material for a new hero-saga.

Even in those early days preceding the migration there were two classes of minstrels, the scops who dwelt in the halls of princes, and the gleemen who wandered. It was by the gleeman, probably, that the news of the disaster of Hrothgar was carried to the realm of Hygelac. Sometimes, to be sure, the scop journeyed to other courts, for such we have found was the habit of Widsith.

The scop was not always so happy as Widsith; sometimes he was deposed in favor of another, and, so retired, lived in disgrace. Such a lot is given to Deor, a scop of the Heodenings, who is made to lament his fate in a little strophic song, the one surviving example of the strophe in Old English. In his sorrow he tries to reassure himself by recalling the heroes of his familiar sagas, who have triumphed over cruel odds— Weland, a fast-bound prisoner to Nithhad; Beadohild, when she discovered her pregnancy; Geat, persecuted with a hard courtship; Theodoric, an exile; and the victims of Eormanric's wolfish soul. Each stanza ends: 'That he overcame, this also may I'. Lastly he mentions his own lot: 'This of myself I will say, that I betimes was Heodening's bard, to my lord dear, I, Deor by name. I had for many winters a goodly retinue, a gracious lord, until Heorrenda now, a man skilled in song, the landright received, which erstwhile the Protection of men had granted me.'[2]

---
[1] Beowulf 2105 ff.   [2] Deor 36 ff.

The allusions in this poem show a close familiarity with the sagas of Weland, of Gudrun, and of Theodoric. This familiarity on the part of the pre-migratory English is substantiated by the fragments of the Battle of Finnsburg and of Waldhere, and by the scop's tale in Beowulf, which is closely related to the former, and recounts the treachery of Finn, and the long struggle of the Frisians and Franks.

The Latin historians were surprised at the fondness of the Germans for the sagas. Tacitus[1] and Jordanes[2] allude to these songs of ancestors, which the Germans sang to the harp, and which served to keep alive their traditions.

By no means did the Germans forget their sagas when they sought the new land, for the complaint of Deor is found in a manuscript of the eleventh century, and the Beowulf continued to be sung even after England was converted, for the Biblical interpolations blend so naturally with the primitive spirit of the tale that the harmony is not disturbed. Rather was the migration a boon to music, for what must have been the wild glee of the Angles and Saxons when they stood in the midst of a new and fertile land, a proud civilization humbled at their feet!

But we must not think that the music of the ancestors of the English was confined to sagas. Choral hymns, enchantments against disease and evil spirits, charms courting the favor of the Gods for the crops, death-lays, bridal-songs, and battle-lays, all these forms are found in the early Germanic music, although they appear less prominently. They too were brought to the new land, and will be discussed later in connection with their Old English descendants.

---

[1] Ann. 2. 88: 'Caniturque (Arminius) adhuc barbaras apud gentes'; Germ. 2: 'Celebrant carminibus antiquis, quod unum apud illos memoriae et annalium genus est, Tuisconem deum terra editum, et filium Mannum, originem gentis conditoresque'; 3: 'Sunt illis haec quoque carmina, quorum relatu, quem barditum vocant, accendunt animos, futuraeque pugnae fortunam ipso cantu augurantur'.

[2] 5: 'Ante quos etiam cantu majorum facta modulationibus citharisque canebant, Ethespamarae, Hanalae, Fridigerni, Widiculae, et aliorum, quorum in hac gente magna opinio est, quales vix heroas fuisse miranda jactat antiquitas.'

New Forces in Music after the Migration.

Scarcely had the Germans made themselves a home, ere new forces entered to influence the music. Christianity came to them, and beautiful is the story of their ready acceptance of a Higher Prince, for they translated into fidelity to him the loyalty to the liege-lord which was a racial trait. Their intensity, ideality, and high regard for woman, found in the self-denying service of Christ, and in the worship of the Virgin, a new and more exalted expression, and one will enquire of history in vain for a more divine and elementally beautiful civilization than the England of the seventh and eighth centuries. Christianity influence both the form and the spirit of the music; it introduced the sweet music of St. Gregory, and it gave rise to new sagas, half Christian and half heathen in conception, in which the great ones of the Lord are the heroes.

Another influence, more difficult to trace, but undoubted, was the contact with the peoples near whom they had settled. Ireland was a land of bards. From the distant centuries, where reality merged in myth, to their own day, the bardic meeting had been a sacred occasion. In that senate the champions of song met, and contended for supremacy in wisdom and music. All Ireland was a training school for this gathering, and song was everywhere. The self-abandoning emotion of the Kelt, and his imagination, with its responsive feeling for nature, found expression and nourishment in his songs. How exalted a place bardism held with the Kelt, we may gather from the words of Talhairan, who points to God as its origin:

'There will be baptism until the day of judgment,
Which (day) will adjudge the character
Of the power of Bardism.
It is He who has bestowed
The great poetic genius and its mystery.'[1]

Can we doubt that the warmth which began to be felt in the Northumbria of the seventh century, and which glows in the writings of Cynewulf, was due to Irish influence? Not if we recall the intercourse between Northumbria and Ireland.

---
[1] 'Bardism in the Sixth Century,' in the Cambrian Journal for 1854.

Despite its fearful intestine troubles, there was unequaled love for learning in Ireland during the seventh and eighth centuries, and thither the English nobility and students went.[1] There were great schools at Iona, at Lismore, and at Clonard; at the monastery of Iona, where the poems of its founder, St. Columba, must have been loved, were educated Oswald, with his princely retinue, Oswy, and Aldfrith. Through the influence of Oswald and Oswy, and their monasteries at Lindisfarne and Whitby, which were modeled after the Irish plan, and filled with Irish monks, all Northumbria drank of Irish knowledge.

Nor was this intercourse confined to the North: Aldhelm speaks of the English youth flocking to Ireland,[2] and he himself left Canterbury in 675 to study under the Irish monk Mailduf, a man of great erudition, in his little hut in the woods, the foundation of Malmesbury.[3] A letter written by Aldhelm to Wilfrid, when the latter was about to leave for Ireland, shows that Ireland was a Mecca for secular, as well as for sacred, studies.[4]

With such intimacy existing between Ireland and England, it would be strange indeed if the English minstrels had not visited the Irish courts. It is significant that we find the *timpan*, a favorite stringed instrument of the Irish bards, in common use in England in the tenth century.[5]

The bitterness which the Welsh felt for the English forbad much intercourse in the seventh century—a bitterness so great that they regarded the Christianity of the English of no avail,[6] and carefully cleansed the plates from which the English had eaten, after throwing the remnants to the dogs and swine.[7] In the centuries succeeding, however, Wales and England drew together; thus in the middle of the eighth century, the Welsh aided Æthelbald of Mercia in warring against Cuthred.[8] In such a camp the Welsh bards must have mingled with the English, and the English must have learned the character of Welsh bardism. According to the Laws

---

[1] Bede 3. 27; Aldhelm, Ep. 3. [2] ibid.
[3] Ep. 5; Bede 5. 18. [4] Ep. 13.
[5] Stubbs, Memorials of Dunstan 79.
[6] Bede 2. 20. [7] Ald. Ep. 1.
[8] Anglo-Saxon Chronicles 752—753.

of Howel Dha, the court had two bards among its twenty-four officers, one the bard of the chair, the other the bard of the household. Both bards were supported bountifully, and sat at the table of the King. At the feasts of Christmas, Easter, and Whitsuntide, the household bard sat next the chief of the household, who placed the harp in his hands. Ordinarily, when song was desired, the bard of the chair sang two songs, the first a song of God, and the second of the King. After him, the bard of the household sang three songs on various subjects. And whenever the queen desired a song, the bard of the household went to her, and sang without limitation.[1]

Moreover, music was an accomplishment of the people at large; Giraldus Cambrensis says that the stranger who came to a Welsh home in the morning hours was entertained with the conversation of maidens and with the music of the harp until evening.[2] The intimacy between Wales and England was close in the ninth century, when many Welsh princes sought the protection of Alfred for their lands. Alfred was fond of the Welsh people; his admirer and biographer, Asser, was a Welshman; and doubtless the royal court of Wessex often rang with the strains of Welsh music.

Giraldus Cambrensis wrote in the twelfth century, and he describes what seems to have been a well-developed system of part-singing among the Welsh, and remarks a similar custom among the Angles in Yorkshire. The following is the passage: 'The Britons do not sing their tunes in unison, like the inhabitants of other countries, but in different parts: so that when a company of singers meet to sing, as is usual in this country, as many different parts are heard as there are singers, who all finally unite in consonance and organic melody, under the softness of B flat. In the northern parts of Britain, beyond the Humber, and on the borders of Yorkshire, the inhabitants make use of a similar kind of symphonious harmony in singing, but with only two differences or varieties of tone and voice, the one murmuring the under part, the other singing the upper in a manner equally soft and pleasing. This they do not so

---

[1] Jones, Williams, and Pughee, Myvyran Archaeology of Wales 1014.
[2] Descriptio Cambriae 1.10.

much by art as by a habit peculiar to themselves, which long practice has made almost natural; and this method of singing has taken such deep root among this people, that hardly any melody is accustomed to be uttered simply or otherwise than in many parts by the former, and in two parts by the latter. And, what is more astonishing, their children, as soon as they begin to sing, adopt the same manner.'[1]

This passage has provoked endless discussion. The defenders of the Welsh musical genius can see but one interpretation, the knowledge of harmony. Several able musical authorities, however, ridicule such an assumption, asserting that Giraldus is full of inaccuracies, and consequently cannot be relied upon in so delicate a question. Yet if Giraldus had not found such music, what suggested the idea of harmony to him? Are we to suppose that he worked out the theory of harmony? To be sure, crude attempts at harmony were made in ecclesiastical music; indeed, vocal accompaniments, known as *organa*, had been practised for a long time, but nothing so mature as Giraldus describes.

Curious specimens of exercises for the harp, supposed to have been composed at a gathering of the Welsh masters of music in 1110, show undoubtedly an appreciation of harmony.[2] And if the crwth, as we have reason to think, underwent little

---

[1] The translation is from Naumann, History of Music, edited by Ouseley, 1. 401; the original Latin from the Descriptio Cambriae, 1. 13, is as follows: 'In musico modulamine, non uniformiter ut alibi, sed multipliciter, multisque modis et modulis, cantilenas emittunt. Adeo ut in turba canentium, sicut huic genti mos est, quot videas capita, tot audias carmina discriminaque vocum varia, in unam denique sub B mollis dulcedine blanda consonantiam, et organicam convenientia melodiam. In borealibus quoque majoris Brittaniae partibus, trans Humbriam scilicet, Eboraci finibus, Anglorum populi, qui partes illas inhabitant, simili canendo symphonica utuntur harmonia: binis tamen solummodo tonorum differentiis, et vocum modulando varietatibus; una inferius submurmurante, altera vero superne demulcente pariter et delectante. Ne arte tamen, sed usu longaevo, et quasi in naturam mora diutina jam converso, haec vel illa sibi gens hanc specialitatem comparavit. Qui adeo apud utramque invaluit, et altas jam radices posuit, ut nihil hic simpliciter, nihil nisi multipliciter ut apud priores, vel saltem dupliciter ut apud sequentes, melice proferri consueverit: pueris etiam, quod magis admirandum, et fere infantibus, cum primum a fletibus in cantus erumpunt, eandem modulationem observantibus.'

[2] Burney, Hist. of Music 112 ff.

change for several centuries, it bears testimony to a knowledge of harmony among the Welsh. As described in the latter part of the Introduction, it has six strings, only two of which can be struck independently. The strings are not tuned in octaves, but as follows:

Ammianus Marcellinus, who visited the Britons in the fourth century, found bardism current among them: 'Bards, indeed, sang the brave deeds of illustrious men in heroic verse, to the sweet strains of the harp'.[1] Similarly Diodorus Siculus: 'There are among them makers of verse, whom they call bards. These, with instruments resembling lyres, praise some in song, and blaspheme others'.[2] So bardism was known to all of the early inhabitants of England, to the Britons who dwelt close to the new-comers, as well as to the Irish and Welsh.

The intercourse between these different peoples and the English must have been attended by a gradual amalgamation of their musical traditions. This blending with new peoples, then, was the second of the forces which conspired to influence English music after the migration.

Secular Music in England.

If we may judge from the fragmentary evidence which has come down to us, the English kings and nobles cherished court music, as their ancestors had done. From his infancy, Alfred was used to hearing the Saxon songs by day and by night, so that he learned them by heart.[3] The customs in his father's

---

[1] 15. 9: 'Et Bardi quidem fortia virorum illustrium facta heroicis composita versibus cum dulcibus lyrae modulis cantitarunt.'

[2] 5. 31: 'Εἰσὶ δε παρ' αὐτοῖς καὶ ποιηταὶ μελῶν, οὓς βάρδους ὀνομάζουσιν. οὗτοι δὲ μετ ὀργάνων ταῖς λύραις ὁμοίων ᾄδοντες, οὓς μὲν ὑμνοῦσιν, οὓς δὲ βλασφημοῦσι.'

[3] Asser, in Mon. Hist. Britt., 473: 'Saxonica poemata die noctuque solens auditor relatu aliorum saepissime audiens, docibilis moriter retinebat.'

court were similar, probably, to those in the court of Charles the Great, where music, or reading of the stories and deeds of olden times, was listened to at the table.¹ Moreover, Charles had the old rude songs of wars and ancient kings written out for transmission to posterity,² and it is interesting to find the stepmother of Alfred, herself a Frankish woman, offering a book of Saxon poems to that one of her sons who would first learn them.³

These lays must have made a deep impression upon Alfred, for they were in harmony with his manliness, and we catch a reflection of their spirit in the courage and persistency which liberated his realm. After peace came, Alfred established schools for the English boys, educating many of them in the court school with his own children, and there special attention was paid to the Saxon poems.⁴ He set a good example for his people by memorizing such poems himself.⁵

How much these poems had changed in tone from the old Teutonic songs we cannot tell, nor can we tell to what extent they were sung, and to what extent recited; but doubtless there were those in the court who sang them. Surely the love for the harp had not died, for in the court of Edmund, the grandson of Alfred, its strains were welcome. Dunstan, who had learned music in his own refined home, often used to divert the mind of Edmund from affairs of state with the music of the *timpan*, or of the harp.⁶

We have reason to suppose that court music was fostered by Cnut, for he wrote many songs himself, some of which were sung by choruses long afterwards.⁷

Among the common people, singing was cherished in the festive gatherings where beer was drunk, and where the harp accompanied the song. Such a gathering Cædmon attended on the night of his memorable vision,⁸ and these occassions must have been common enough among a people to whom the inability to play and sing was a disgrace. It

---

¹ Eginhard, Vita Karoli c. 24.   ² ibid. c. 29.
³ Asser 474.   ⁴ ibid. 485 ff.   ⁵ ibid. 486.
⁶ Stubbs, Mem. of Dunst. 79.
⁷ Hist. Eliensis 2. 27, in Gale, Hist. Scrip. 1. 505.
⁸ Bede 4, 24.

was in just such gatherings of the people, and from just such inventiveness as Cædmon showed, that the old sagas took on their new matter, as each man sang in turn. Who can say that our ancestors would not have sung an epic as exalted as the Odyssey, if Christianity had not entered to dissipate the productive power of epic poetry? The fondness for the songs was not lost even by those who gave themselves to the service of the church. Cuthbert says that Bede was 'skilled in our songs'.[1] Aldhelm used to disguise himself as a minstrel and to take his stand on a bridge, that he might, by his songs, gain the ear of the people, and then teach them the truth.[2] Indeed William of Malmesbury says that one of Aldhelm's ballads was a favorite in his day, four hundred years after.[3] The compositions of Artwil, the son of an Irish king, were submitted to Aldhelm for correction.[4] Dunstan, the lover and ecclesiastical zealot, was proficient in music, and was fond of making musical instruments. A pretty story is told by his first biographer, the unknown Auctor B, and copied by the others, of an Aeolian harp which he had made. Once he called upon a woman to suggest a design for an embroidered robe; as he was intent upon the work, suddenly his harp began to play sweetly, and the surprised maidens who were assisting him heard in its strains a sweet and perfect anthem. This of course was before he became an ecclesiastic.[5] In his love for musical instruments, and in his fineness of nature as well, Dunstan reminds us of that Tutilo of St. Gall, who used to make instruments with great skill, and who had a school, in connection with the monastery, where he taught the art of playing musical instruments to the sons of nobles.[6] Bernlef, the blind Frisian, who visited the English, was loved by every one because he could sing the old legends so sweetly.[7] The use which was made of the harp and other instruments in worship tended to perpetuate secular music among the ecclesiastics.

---

[1] Migne, Patrologia Latina 90. 40.
[2] Mabillon, Act. SS. 3. 224.
[3] Malm., Gesta Pontificum 336.   [4] ibid. 336.
[5] Stubbs, Mem. of Dunst. 21.
[6] Ekkehart, Casus S. Galli 3, in Mon. Germ. Hist. 2.
[7] Vita S. Liudgeri 2. 1, in Mon. Germ. Hist. 2.

As time went on, the English gleemen, in common with the gleemen upon the continent, lessened the dignity of their art, by identifying themselves with buffoons, jugglers, and tumblers. Manuscripts of the later Old English times are illuminated with drawings, representing people dancing, or juggling balls and knives, to the music of the double pipe, fiddle, or harp, and, what is most significant, these performers are frequently the attendants of King David. Fondness for this revelry was one of the causes which led to the disastrous decadence among the clergy. Consequently, in the monastic revival instituted by Æthelwold and Dunstan, such licence was denied the priest. It speaks volumes for the religious degeneracy of the times that laws, forbidding the priests to be buffoons and ale-bards, were necessary.[1]

Wulfstan, the sombre prophet, whose words came to the English like the utterances of Jeremiah to the Jews, warning them of the wrath to come, condemned the beer-halls, with their harps and pipes and merriment, and saw the day fast approaching, when the ears would be dull which had been full ready to hear fair music and songs.[2] Occasional references in religious writings to the lewd and devilish songs of the world argue a close and corrupt social atmosphere. How much that was low had crept in we cannot tell, but coarseness is always present when the dignity of social life yields to the absurd and jocose.

And yet there were not wanting those who loved the old, pure song, and who kept it alive in the homes. We have seen how large a place it had in Alfred's home, and when Thomas à Becket[3] went to Paris, in 1159, to propose a marriage between the royal houses, he entered the French towns 'preceded by two hundred and fifty boys on foot, in groups of six, ten, or more together, singing English songs, according to the custom of their country'.

It was a Teutonic custom for the warriors to rush into battle dancing and shouting a wild war-song, while the spears and shields were struck together in mad accompaniment. The

---

[1] Canons of Edgar 58. Laws of the Northumbrian Priests 41.
[2] Wulfstan, Homilies 148. 3.
[3] Thomas Becket, Rolls Series 3. 31.

song commenced with a distinguishable chant to the glory of some great fighter, and ended in a hoarse tumult of excited voices. The women, assembled near the contestants, fired their spirit by continuing the noise, and by appealing to the bravery of their husbands and children.¹

That this custom was perpetuated by the Old English is shown by the existence of such words as *fyrdlēoð, gūðlēoð, hildelēoð,* and *wīglēoð.* To be sure, for the most part these words are used in a figurative sense—thus the wolf or the eagle sings the war-song as the army advances,² and the trumpet sounds it before them,³—yet this figurative use emphasizes the close association of martial music with the onslaught. And we have other satisfactory evidence of the existence of the war-song. In the Judith, as the warriors pour out of the city, they strike their shields and spears together, in accordance with the old custom,⁴ and in the Exodus a song of victory is raised when the exiles see the Egyptians perish in the sea.⁵

It may have been a Teutonic custom to have some famous singer go before the army, as was the custom among the later Germans.⁶ It was in such a way that the Normans entered the battle of Hastings. Taillefer, a minstrel and warrior, rode before the army, tossing his sword in the air and catching it again, while he chanted a song of Roland.⁷

---

¹ Tacitus, Hist. 2. 22: 'Cantu truci et moro patrio nudis corporibus super humeros scuta quatientium'; Ann. 4. 47: 'Simul in ferocissimos, qui ante vallum, more gentis, cum carminibus et tripudiis persultabant'; Germ. 3: 'Fuisse apud eos et Herculem memorant, primumque omnium virorum fortium ituri in proelia canunt. Sunt illis haec quoque carmina, quorum relatu, quem barditum vocant, accendunt animos, futuraeque pugnae fortunam ipso cantu augurantur; terrent enim trepidantve, prout sonuit acies, nec tam vocis ille quam virtutis concentus videtur. Adfectatur praecipue asperitas soni et fractum murmur, objectis ad os scutis, quo plenior et gravior vox repercussu intumescat'; 7: It is interesting to find that the custom of the Gauls was similar, thus Livy 38. 17. 4: 'Cantus ineuntium proelium, et ululatus et tripudia'.
² Elene 27, and Judith 211.   ³ Exod. 221.
⁴ 204 ff.   ⁵ Exod. 577.
⁶ Paul, Grundriss 2. 1. 166: 'Vielfach mag auch, wie in späterer Zeit sicher, ein Vorsänger vorhanden gewesen sein: Ludw. 46: "Ther kuning reit knono, sang lioth frano, ioh alle saman sungun."'
⁷ Wace, Le Roman de Rou:

The various ceremonies of the funeral were among the most stubborn of heathen remains. To the time of the Normans, the church was not able fully to overcome the hold which the Teutonic dirges had upon the people of England. In the tenth century, the priests were instructed to forbid the heathen songs of the laymen and their loud cachinnations.[1] One of the weighty charges brought against Dunstan by his young rivals at the court was that he loved frivolous songs and funeral dirges.[2] The Irish, with whom the English were so familiar, kept up their wailings for the dead, which were notably violent,[3] and so helped to perpetuate the custom among the English.

Similar obstinacy was encountered by the German ecclesiastics. Indeed the funeral customs of the Indo-Europeans tended to perpetuate themselves with very little change. The earliest description of these customs in European literature is in the Iliad. The body of Hector was placed upon a bed of state, and beside it gathered the 'minstrels, leaders of the dirge', and the woman to wail with them. Andromache and Hekabe and Helen, each in turn, uttered a lament over the body. Then the funeral pyre was built, the body was burned, and a mound of stones was piled above it.[4] While the body of Achilles was being burned the mail-clad warriors, on horse and afoot, moved about the pyre with a great noise.[5] Then a feast was held. The funeral of Severus, described by Herodian,

---

        Sur un cheval ki tost alloit
        Devant li Ducs alloit cantant
        De Karlemaine et de Rollant
        Et d'Oliver e des vassals
        Qui moururent en Renchevals.

[1] Canons of Ælfric 35.

[2] Stubbs, Mem. of Dunst. 11: 'Dicentes illum ex libris salutaribus et viris peritis, non saluti animarum profutura sed avitae gentilitatis vanissima didicisse carmina, et historiarum frivolas colere incantationum naenias.'

[3] Giraldus Cambrensis, Topogr. Hibernica 1. 12: 'Est itaque tanquam convertibilis musica naturae. Hujus enim opera, animum si intendis, incendis; si remittis, amittis. Unde et gens Hibernica et Hispanice, aliaeque nationes nonnullae, inter lugubres funerum planctus musicas efferunt lamentationes: quatinus vel dolorem instantem augeant et recentem, vel forte ut minuant jam remissum'.

[4] Iliad 24. 719 ff.   [5] Odyssey 24. 68 ff.

differed only in detail from the Greek funeral. The body was buried, but a likeness of it was treated as a less artificial people would have treated the body itself. This effigy was placed upon a richly ornamented bed of state, physicians attended it, and finally pronounced it dead. Then boys and girls from the nobility sang dirges beside it. Thence the body was taken to the Campus Martius, and placed in a pyramidal structure decked with gifts. Then this structure was set on fire, and the Roman knights rode around it. The following days were devoted to games and feasts.[1]

We have descriptions of Germanic funerals closely resembling these. At the funeral of Attila games were held, and then about the body, placed in the midst of a plain, the best horsemen from all the Huns rode, and sang of his possessions and valor.[2] The body of Beowulf was placed upon a high pyre, laden with treasures, the people wailed around it, and the widow sang a woful lay. Then at the edge of a bluff overlooking the sea was raised a barrow, into which were thrown bracelets and rings, and around this rode twelve sons of nobles, who bemoaned their lord and chanted an elegy.[3] Similarly in the lay of Hnæf, related by Hrothgar's minstrel, his mother wept upon his shoulder, and uttered dirges.[4] A very dramatic picture is found, in one of the stories related by Beowulf, of the old man who is compelled to deny his son the blessing of burial: 'So it is a sad thing for an aged man to bear, that his boy rides young on the gallows. Then he wails a dirge, a song of sorrow, while his son hangs a joy to ravens, and him he may not help, he old and stricken in years.'[5]

There are nine words in Old English which mean a funeral songe or dirge, and with such etymological signi-

---

[1] Herodian 4.
[2] Jordanes 49. The dirge was as follows: 'Praecipuus Hunorum rex Attila, patre genitus Mundzucco, fortissimarum gentium dominus, qui inaudita ante se potentia solus Scythica et Germanica regna possedit, nec non utraque Romani orbis imperia captis civitatibus terruit, et ne praedae reliqua subderentur placatus precibus annuum vectigal accepit: cumque haec omnia proventu felicitatis egerit, non vulnere hostium, non fraude suorum, sed in gente incolume inter gaudia laetus sine sensu doloris occubuit. Quis ergo hunc exitum putet quem nullus aestimat vindicantum.'
[3] Beowulf 3110 ff.   [4] ibid. 1117.   [5] ibid. 2444 ff.

ficances as *burial-song* and *body-song*, there could be little doubt, even without the recorded opposition of the church, of the presence of the heathen funeral customs. It may be that some of these dirges were to be sung over the graves of the dead, in accordance with the ancestor-worship of the Teutons.[1] Doubtless the 'incantations and charms and mysteries of the hellish art', of which Bede complains,[2] were the enchantments and death dances by which it was hoped to restore life.[3]

Music also formed an essential of the marriage festivities, as the expressive words *brȳdsang*, *brȳdlēoð*, and *giftlēoð*, indicate. The Old English literature, in itself, throws little light upon marriage rites, but the German supplements it well. Kögel[4] has gathered comprehensive evidence, and shows that the Germanic customs differed little from the early Greek as described in the lines on the shield of Achilles: 'Also he fashioned therein two fair cities of mortal men. In the one were espousals and marriage feasts, and beneath the blaze of torches they were leading the brides from their chambers through the city, and lovely arose the bridal song. And young men were whirling in the dance, and among them flutes and viols sounded high; and the women standing each at her door were marveling.[5] The Germanic bridal song was probably sung, as in this Greek wedding, while the bride, surrounded by dancers, was being led to her new home.[6] The supposition that such a procession formed a part of the service among the early English, as well as among the Germans, is supported by the word *brȳdlāc*, for the primary idea of *lāc*, as of the Old High German *leich*, is motion.[7] It is easy to believe that music was a prominent part of a wedding of such splendor as is suggested by Asser in his life of Alfred.[8]

---

[1] Gummere, Germanic Origins cap. 2.
[2] Bede 4. 27.
[3] Der Totenkranz, in Lachmann, Kleinere Schriften.
[4] Paul, Grundriss 2. 1. 105 ff.
[5] Lang, Leaf and Myers, Iliad 381.
[6] Lex Salica 13. 10. app. 4: 'Si quis puella sponsata ducte ducente in via adsallierit'; Weinhold; Die deutschen Frauen in dem Mittelalter 1. 390: 'Sus giengin die jungin hupfinde unde springinde, von den brūtin singinde, einander werfinde den bal.'
[7] Grimm, Deut. Myth. 35.   [8] Asser, Mon. Hist. Britt. 484.

A most interesting store of incantations, part heathen and part Christian in character, is contained in the Old English charms. There were charms against all sorts of opposing spirits, against the Mighty Women, against storms, and against disease. There were charms to be sung to Mother Earth in the Spring, when the soil was consecrated at the altar, charms invoking the aid of Fire or Water, and others that introduced Woden. The traditionary wealth of the race was bound up in these charms, and to analyze them would be to analyze Teutonic mythology. The church at first adopted these heathen rites, by mixing them with others of its own, but later opposed violently those that had not become decidedly Christian in character.[1]

Ecclesiastical Music in England.

Worthy to be cherished is the picture of that April morning, and the little band of Christians as they followed the tall, grave Augustine, beneath the banner of Christ, down into the village of Canterbury, through the company of English, awed by the presaging strains of the Rogation Anthem: 'We beseech Thee, O Lord, for thy great mercy, let Thine anger and wrath be turned away from this city, and from Thy holy house, for we have sinned, Alleluia!'[2] The majesty, the brightness, and the tenderness, of the new faith, and the simple sweet lives of its advocates, could not be resisted. Æthelbert, the King of Kent, was baptized on Whitsun-eve, the first of June, and ten thousand of his men on the following Christmas. So the flower of Christianity blossomed in Kent almost before the seed was planted.

The Gregorian music was used from the first, in Kent, as the only orthodox course. Putta, who was made bishop of Rochester in 669, had learned music from 'the disciples of the Holy Pope Gregory', and Maban, who went to teach music to the brethren at Hexham in 709, had learned it 'from

---

[1] For these charms see Cockayne, Leechdoms; for discussion, Gummere, Germ. Orig. caps. 13—14, Brooke, Eng. Lit. fr. the Beginning to the Norm. Conq. 44 ff., Paul, Grundriss 2. 1. 160 ff.
[2] Bede, Eccl. Hist. 1. 25.

the successors of the disciples of the Holy Pope Gregory'. These 'disciples' were, of course, the missionaries of Augustine.

It has been usual of late years to question, if not to deny, the connection of Pope Gregory the First with the music which bears his name, and to date the origin of the music a century later. Such is the theory upheld by Batiffol, a careful student of the Breviary.[1] However, Bäumer, a Benedictine, has met the arguments of Batiffol, and shows, beyond any reasonable doubt, that Gregory was behind the Gregorian music, and that he established a school of music.[2]

Nauman has summed up the main characteristics of the Gregorian music in the following passage: 'The chant, as now arranged by Gregory, differed from the Ambrosian in that it was no longer recited, nor governed by the length or quantity of the syllables or the metre of the language, but consisted of continuous melodies, the length of each tone differing but slightly in value. It possessed something of that peculiarly impressive character belonging to the church chorale, so adequately fitted for its divine purpose, partaking of that seriousness and majestic dignity which makes the chorale a fit offering to Him who is far above time, space, and the accidents of every-day life.

'The Gregorian chant was termed *Cantus planus* or *Cantus choralis*. The first name was given to it on account of the even, measured movement of its melody, the second term, *Cantus choralis*, signifying that the melody was not to be sung by a single person, but by the chorus or congregation. The participation of the latter, however, was somewhat limited, as Gregory directed that it should be chiefly sung by the duly appointed choirs. The Gregorian chant also received the name *Canonicus*, because all liturgical texts were provided with special melodies that were to be used by the united church as canonical, and hence arose the term of *Cantus firmus*—i. e., fixed chant.—Gregory added to the four Ambrosian scales, known as the *Authentic*, four others which received the name of *Plagal*, or oblique. The latter he constructed by prefacing each *original* scale with its last four tones—e. g., in the first scale (*D—D*) the four final tones are *A, B, C, D*; these he

---

[1] Hist. du Bréviaire romain.   [2] Bäumer, Gesch. d. Breviers.

placed an octave lower, at the same time putting them before the initial note of the scale, viz., *D*. The new scale thus formed ranged from *A* to *A*, and the whole eight scales, i. e., the four Authentic and the four Plagal, were then called *Church modes*, and written as follows:—

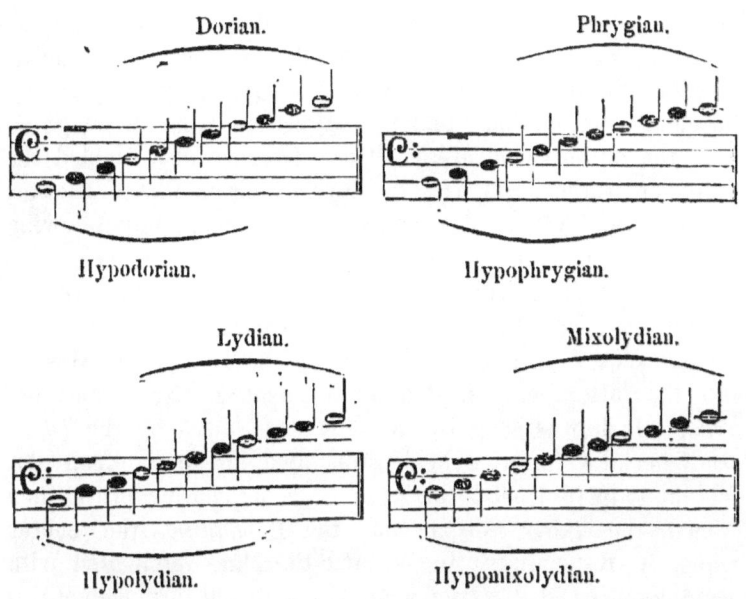

'It will be noticed that the initial note of the Authentic scale becomes the fourth note of the Plagal Scale. The latter scale appears to stride upwards to attain its fourth tone, feeling this to be its true basis (notwithstanding in theory its *initial* note would be its *groundtone*); and in a like manner does the Authentic scale recognise in this one and the same tone its first and groundnote. This will explain why the melodies of the Plagal scales have their movement upwards, and why those of the Authentic, always returning to their base note, have the character of rest.

'It is undeniable that the Authentic melodies possess a sensuous charm capable of inducing deep religious fervour. A somewhat similar feeling, however, is engendered by Plagal melodies, because of the aversion to construct melodies on scales which have a semitone between the seventh and eighth,

2*

the seventh of all Plagal scales (with the exception of the sixth from *C* to *C*) being a full tone below the octave. Only one other of the eight Gregorian Church modes, viz., the fifth (from *F* to *F*), possessed a leading note. Even when melodies were based on these two Church modes the semitone was often avoided. Again, the strong dislike of employing the third of the tonic, especially in ascending passages, invests Gregorian melodies with an undeniable mystical (?) character.

'The Gregorian system was now generally adopted by Christian congregations, and new directions were promulgated as to the performance of the Mass. Gregory also divided the *Kyrie* into three parts, viz., the Kyrie Eleison, Christe Eleison, repeating the Kyrie as the third section. Immediately following the Kyrie came the *Hymnus Angelicus* (known to-day as the *Gloria in excelsis*), which was then succeeded by the Collects or Orations for the priest. The *Graduale*, *Alleluia*, and *Sequentia* were then inserted between the Epistle and Gospel, both the latter being recited by the deacon. Next came the *Credo*, which was sung by the chorus, followed by the *Offertory* (special Offertories being appointed for special festivals), and the *Sanctus* and *Benedictus*. The officiating priest then intoned the *Pater Noster* and the *Communio*, the chorus frequently responding 'Amen', and the Mass terminated with the *Agnus Dei* and *Dona nobis pacem*. The arrangement of the Mass as it then stood has remained unchanged to the present day, and has been the groundwork on which some of the noblest musical compositions have been raised into monuments of imperishable grandeur.'[1]

As the above passage suggests, the singing was confined, at first, too much to the choir. To obviate this, sequences, to be sung by the congregation, were introduced. These followed the Kyrie, Jubilus, and Alleluia, and were so popular that they expanded until they included whole hymns.

Gregory was careful to have some of the singers, trained in his school, included in the little company of Augustine. A school for teaching music and sacred lore was established by these men at Canterbury in the early part of the seventh century, for in 631 Felix founded a school, after the model of Kent, at Dunwich, among the East Angles.[2]

---

[1] Ouseley-Naumann, Hist. of Music 184 ff. [2] Bede 3. 18.

Introduction. 21

The spread of the Gregorian music was slow, outside of the southern district centering about Canterbury. The Irish missionaries in Northumbria, without any question, would use the course of music familiar to the Irish church. It is not known what that music was.[1] Unfortunately a work, De Cantu, by St. Columba, a noted devotee of music, is lost. Whatever the Irish service may have been, it was intoned, for the word 'decantare' is used of the introduction of the Liturgy into Ireland in the fifth century, and it is said of St. Columba that he might be heard a mile when chanting.[2] The Irish missionaries to Northumbria had been disciples of St. Colomba at Iona, and the Irish course must have got well rooted in the North of England.

However, after the defeat of the Irish and Scotic parties at the Council of Whitby in 664, the Gregorian music spread rapidly. James the Deacon, who was 'extraordinarily skillful in singing', had been at York with Paulinus, and when the latter was made bishop of Rochester in 633, James took charge of the church at York. There 'he rescued much prey from the power of the old enemy of mankind', and 'when the province was afterwards restored to peace, he began to teach many of the church to sing, according to the custom of the Romans, or of the Cantuarians.'[3] His teaching, however, was confined to the church at York. But when Wilfrith returned to the North in 669, he took with him Eddi and Æona, skillful singers, whom he had met at Canterbury, while studying the Benedictine Rule there. They went about among the churches, and 'trained choirs to sing responsively, according to the customs of the primitive church'.[4]

Eddi and Æona did not visit the extreme North, but when Benedict Biscop and Ceolfrith were in Rome in 680, they besought the Pope to send John, the precentor of St. Peters and a skillfull singer, to Wearmouth. The Pope granted the request, and John returned with them, gathering some assistants in Gaul by the way. John visited many of the neighboring churches, and scholars were sometimes sent to him for training.[5]

---
[1] Sullivan-O'Curry, Manners and Customs of the Early Irish J. 511 ff.
[2] Reeve's Adamnan 1. 37.
[3] Bede 2. 20.   [4] Eddi 45, Bede 4. 2.   [5] Bede 4. 18.

How much his labors were appreciated we may judge from a pathetic incident which attended the plague in 686. All the brothers at Jarrow who could chant the anthems and responses were swept away, except Ceolfrith and a small boy, by some supposed to have been Bede. Reluctantly the abbot told the little lad that the psalms would have to be recited, unaccompanied by the anthems. For a week they went through the offices in this way, the tears of Ceolfrith often interrupting. Then he could stand it no longer, and the services were recited in full by the abbot and the child, until Ceolfrith could train, or could procure, proper associates.[1]

In 709 when Acca succeeded Wilfrith at Hexham, he invited Maban, a man trained at Canterbury, to take charge of the music. Maban complied, and established a school of music at Hexham, doubtless modelled after Canterbury. According to Bede's account, Acca 'kept him twelve years, to teach such ecclesiastical songs as were not known, and to restore those to their former state, which were corrupted, either by want of use, or through neglect.'[2]

When Theodore and Hadrian came to Canterbury in 669, they reestablished the school, which had degenerated, and taught all branches of secular and sacred knowledge. Through Canterbury England became the centre of learning for Western Europe. One of the pupils was Aldhelm, who became a brilliant scholar, and attracted many disciples to his Monastery at Malmesbury. He was a famous poet and musician, as has been noted above, and of course established the Gregorian music in the West. William of Malmesbury describes the return of Aldhelm from Rome, when he was greeted by the processional chant.[3] The ecclesiastical music was carried almost to the Welsh border by Putta, who went to Hereford after the destruction of Rochester. There he spent his time in giving instruction in music to the churches.[4] So by the end of the seventh century the music of St. Gregory was well known throughout England.

During the season of ecclesiastical decay, which began in the middle of the eighth century, and which was not properly

---

[1] Stevenson, Bedae Opera Hist. Min. 326.
[2] Bede, 5. 20; transl. by Bohn.
[3] Gesta Pont. 373.   [4] Bede 4. 2, 12.

checked until the monastic revival, little mention is made of church music; it shared a like fate with the other activities of the church.

Under Æthelwulf, the weak-willed King, who was really governed by Ealhstan, the bishop of Sherburne, and by Swithun, the church gained temporal power. He was a sovereign fond of richness, and when he returned to England, after having witnessed the magnificent ceremonies at Rome, he may have taken some interest in elaborating the service at home.

But the church received little substantial aid until Alfred ascended the throne. His efforts to reform and to enlighten his people are familiar to everyone. Churches were rebuilt, monasteries established, foreign scholars and ecclesiastics were summoned, and he himself made translations of some of the significant Latin works. Among the able men who came to his assistance was Grimbald, the chanter, from among the Franks. Asser describes him as: 'indeed a venerable man, a most excellent chanter, well informed in every phase of ecclesiastical discipline, and in the inspired writings, and adorned with all good usages'.[1] The labors of such men as Grimbald, supplemented by the solicitude of the King, and in harmony with the growing confidence of the people, did much to restore the purity and sincerity of the ecclesiastical functions.

But the work which Alfred and his assistants had commenced was not completed by his successors. Renewed political troubles engaged the attention of the kings and dispirited the people, and indifference and vice rushed in to claim their prerogatives. Of course learning and the schools disappeared, so that Ælfric could say, 'before Archbishop Dunstan and Bishop Æthelwold re-established the monastic schools, no English priest could write, or understand, a Latin letter'.

In the glorious company of the revivalists Ælfric himself must be included. These four patriots and men of God, Dunstan, Æthelwold, Oswald, and Ælfric, possessed of a catholicity of view that enabled them to transcend their sur-

---

[1] Asser, Mon. Hist. Britt. 486: 'venerabilem videlicet virum, cantatorem optimum, et omni modo ecclesiasticis disciplinis, et in divina scriptura eruditissimum, et in multis aliis artibus artificiosum'.

roundings, introduced, into the vileness of the church, the pure waters of monasticism. The monasteries were of the order of St. Benedict. The new monasteries adopted the Benedictine service unchanged, the older ones had been following the rules of independent continental orders. To procure uniform use, Æthelwold compiled a rule, largely Benedictine, but modified by previously-existing customs. The monasteries were provided with choirs, in accordance with the Gregorian music, and the services of the Canonical Hours were largely musical.

We find, even in this pre-Norman use, the germs of the dramatic features in church service, which developed into the miracle plays. 'On Easter-day, the seven Canonical Hours were to be sung in the manner of the Canons; and in the night, before Matins, the Sacrists [because our Lord rested in the tomb] were to put the Cross in its place. Then, during a religious service, four Monks robed themselves, one of whom in an alb, as if he had somewhat to do, came stealingly to the tomb, and there holding a palm branch, sat still, till the responsory was ended; then the three others, carrying censers in their hands, came up to him, step by step, as if looking for something. As soon as he saw them approach, he began singing in a soft voice, "Whom seek ye?" to which was replied by the three others in chorus, "Jesus of Nazareth". This was answered by the other, "He is not here, he is risen". At which words, the three last, turning to the choir, cried, "Alleluia, the Lord is risen". The other then, as if calling them back, sang, "Come and see the place"; and then rising, raised the cloth, showed them the place without the Cross, and linen cloths in which it was wrapped. Upon this they laid down their censers, took the cloths, extended them to show that the Lord was risen, and singing an anthem, placed them upon the altar.'[1]

The good work of Dunstan and his colleagues so revitalized religion in England that the church was able to withstand the opposition of the Danes, and even to win the allegiance of Cnut. And this spiritual intensity lasted until the reign of the lethargic Harold. Then the church slept, until the Normans awoke it.

---

[1] Fosbroke, British Monachism, 35 f.

A poem written by Aldhelm, upon the dedication of a certain nunnery, proves that stringed instruments were used in the English church services in the seventh century.[1] A letter written by Cuthbert to Lullus, a German bishop, urging him to send a citharist to Cuthbert, as he has a cithara and cannot play it, is perhaps expressive of Cuthbert's desire to have instruments used in worship.[2] That instruments were connected with worship in the earlier centuries is apparent from the writings to the church fathers.[3] It would seem that the use had not died out in Ælfric's day, for he defines *psalmus* as *hearpsang*, and *canticum* as *psalm æfter hearpsang*; however these translations may be simply reminiscent of a passage from Cassiodorus, where he makes a similar distinction.[4]

Aldhelm also describes an organ with gilt pipes used in worship.[5] Supplementary evidence proves that organs were well known by the English in Aldhelm's day. In 963 an organ with four hundred pipes was erected at Winchester.[6] It may be that other instruments, such as the fiddle and pipes, were used to accompany ecclesiastical music, for the Old English Manuscripts represent David surrounded by men playing various instruments.

Indeed, it would not be surprising if a good deal of festivity, from the pre-Christian worship, lingered in the

---

[1] See p. 31.   [2] See p. 41.

[3] See the discussion of musical insts. in the latter part of the Introduction.

[4] Migne, Patrologia Latina 70. 15 f.: 'Quod sit psalmus: Psalmus est cum ex ipso solo instrumento musico, id est psalterio, modulatio quaedam dulcis et canora profunditur.

Quod sit canticum: Canticum est quod ad honorem Dei canitur, quando quis libertate vocis propriae utitur, nec loquaci instrumento cuiquam musico consona modulatione sociatur, hoc est quod etiam nunc in Divinitatis laudibus agitur.

Quod sit psalmocanticum: Psalmocanticum erat, cum, instrumento musico praecinente, canens chorus sociatis vocibus acclamabat, divinis duntaxat sermonibus obsecutus.

Quod sit canticum psalmum: Canticum psalmum erat, cum, choro ante canente, ars instrumenti musici in unam convenientiam communiter aptabatur, verbaque hymni divini suavis copula personabat.

[5] See p. 46.   [6] ibid.

services, especially in the less conspicuous sections, where more freedom was allowed. The custom of taking sods into church to have masses sung over them, in order that the earth might be fruitful, suggests the possibility of greater freedom. At the return of Aldhelm,[1] the people danced about him in glee, while a processional chant was being sung. Perhaps they were accustomed to dance before the altar, as their ancestors had done.

Music is invariably the phenomenon employed to give expression to the ecstacy and joy of Heaven. The glorious assembly of the angels before the throne are ever praising God, the thought of joining this choral band cheers the saint enduring persecution, and, at his death, angels bear his soul to Heaven, with music ineffable. The vision of the companions of Andrew gives expression to this idea:

'A sleep came o'er us, weary of the sea,
And eagles came across the seething waves
In flight, exulting in their mighty wings,
And while we slept they took our souls away;
With joy they bore us, flying through the air,
Gracious and bright, rejoicing in their speed.
Gently they caressed us, while they sang
Continual praise; there was unceasing song
Throughout the sky; a beauteous host was there,
A glorious multitude. The angels stood
About the Prince, the thanes about their Lord,
In thousands; in the highest they gave praise
With holy voice unto the Lord of Lords;
The angel-band rejoiced. We there beheld
The holy Patriarchs, and a mighty troop
Of martyrs; to the Lord victorious
That righteous throng sang neverending praise;
And David too was with them, Jesse's son,
The King of Israel, blessed warrior,
Come to Christ's throne. Likewise we saw you twelve
All standing there before the Son of God,
Glorious men, of great nobility;
Archangels holy, throned in majesty,

---

[1] See p. 22.

Did serve you; happy is it for the man
Who may enjoy that bliss. High joy was there,
Glory of warriors, an exalted life,
Nor was there sorrow there for any man.
Drear exile, open torment is the lot
Of him who must be stranger to these joys,
And wander wretched, when he goes from hence.'[1]

Another account of heavenly music is contained in Owini's story of the angelic spirits who came to tell Chad of his death. 'One day when he (Owini) was thus employed abroad, and his companions were gone to the church, as I began to state, the bishop (Chad) was alone reading or praying in the oratory of that place, when on a sudden, as he afterwards said, he heard the voice of persons singing most sweetly and rejoicing, and appearing to descend from heaven. Which voice he said he first heard coming from the south-east, and that afterwards it drew near him, till it came to the roof of the oratory where the bishop was, and entering therein, filled the same and all about it. He listened attentively to what he heard, and after about half an hour, perceived the same song of joy to ascend from the roof of the said oratory, and to return to heaven the same way it came, with inexpressible sweetness'.[2]

This confounding of music with rapturous experience, is embodied in the very words which denote it. *Dream* means not only music and harmony, but primarily ecstacy and rapture, *mirigness* comes to mean music, by first meaning pleasantness and sweetness, and *gidd* links mirth and song together. The relatively large number of words which mean *melody* and *harmony*, show how prominent music was in the thought of the early English; and such words as *efenhleodor* (*even-* or *equal-sounding*), and *swinsung* and *mirigness*, leave little doubt as to their discrimination between harmony and melody.

---

[1] Andreas, ll. 862—891, trans. by Root.
[2] Bede 4. 3, trans. by Bohn.

Musical Instruments.

Musical instruments may be divided into three classes, stringed instruments, wind instruments and instruments of percussion. Each of these classes finds its representatives among the Old English. To the first class belong the harp, the crwth or crowd, the rotta or rote, the timpan, the fiddle, the psaltery, and perhaps the lyre and cithara. To the second class belong the organ, the bagpipe, the reed-pipe, the double-pipe, the shawm, the horns, and the straight and curved trumpets. To the third class belong the various kinds of bells, the tabor, the cymbals, the *cymbalum*, and possibly a curious brazen instrument known as the bombulum.

The sources, from which I have determined the existence of these instruments, are, the incidental references in the secular texts of the English, Welsh, Irish, French, and Germans, the occasional, though usually unsatisfactory, descriptions in secular writings, the careful descriptions in ecclesiastical writings, and the illuminations in the manuscripts. The illuminations I have not seen, and, consequently, have been compelled to rely upon the reproductions in the various archæological journals, and in such compilations as Westwood's Facsimiles.

There is a surprising correspondence between these descriptions of musical instruments, in the church fathers, and the illuminations. Oftentimes the latter are mechanical and servile attempts to picture the former. For instance, a favorite homiletic illustration with the church fathers, from Augustine to Rabanus Maurus and Pseudo-Bede, was the distinction between the cithara and the psaltery. These instruments, as used by the early Roman church, were quite different in character, the psaltery being square, and the cithara being the classic instrument, with the quadrangular or semiovoid body, and the curving arms. The psaltery had its resonance at the top, whereas, in the cithara, the chamber was at the bottom. It was this distinction that the homilists liked to point out, for, whereas the cithara sounded of the earth, earthy, the psaltery partook of the purity and exaltation of heaven. In course of time, a triangular stringed instrument came to be known as the cithara, and also as the psaltery. A certain monk, who knew of this latter instrument, and who also was mindful of the distinction made by the ecclesiastical writers, illuminated his manuscript with two musical instruments, the first was this triangular instrument, which he called a cithara, the second was the same instrument turned upside down, which he called a psaltery.

Nor can these descriptions themselves be relied upon too implicitly, for some of them are fanciful; thus the wind instrument which had a big pipe for a body, and twelve little pipes leading out of it. This typifies Christ and the disciples, for just as when one blows in the main pipe and the smaller ones resound, so God inspired Christ, and he, the twelve.

Another difficulty is occasioned by the confusion of the names of instruments, a confusion that becomes more troublesome, as the nations become more intimate. Thus cithara, means, sometimes the harp, sometimes the rote, sometimes the triangular psaltery. Indeed very few ninth century instruments are known by the same names in the fourteenth century.

The Harp.

Foremost among Old English instruments is the harp. The antiquity of the harp, dating back at least to the fourth dynasty of the Egyptians, is a familiar fact. How or when it came to the Germanic peoples we do not know, but it was their most common stringed instrument. Enthusiastic mention of it is made in the earliest literature, the Eddic Voluspa and the Beowulf. It was recognised as the Germanic instrument by early historians, thus, in the sixth century, Venantius Fortunatus wrote:

'Romanusque lyra, plaudat tibi barbarus harpa,
Graecus achilliaca, chrotta Britanna canat.'[1]

To the Old English the harp was the glee-beam and the joy-wood.[2] It was the common instrument in the meed-hall, and in the gatherings of the humbler people, and the lot of the man whose wanderings forbad him to listen to its music was hard.[3] By the tenth century, at least, it was used in religious services, and it is significant that, in manuscripts of

---

[1] Ad Lupum Ducem.
[2] *Glīgbēam* and *Gomenwudu* in Glossary.
[3] *Hearpe* in Glossary.

this and the following century, the harp takes the place of the psaltery as the instrument of David. A glance at the relatively large number of words connected with the harp is convincing of its popularity.[1]

Excellent representations of the harp are found. The most ornate and shapely drawing is in a St. Blaise Ms. of the ninth century, where it is called 'cithara anglica'.[2] In the Ms. Cotton, Tiberius C. 6, David is playing a harp of good construction,[3] and another illumination, evidently copied after this, is in the Ms. Ff. 1, 23 of the Cambridge Library.[4] In the former, the harp is played with the fingers, in the latter, the psalmist holds a plectrum in his left hand. Several words meaning *plectrum* are found in Old English,[5] and doubtless the harp was played, sometimes with the plectrum, and sometimes without it. In one of the eleventh century Mss., Claudian B. 4, is a drawing of a man dancing, and, at the same time, playing upon a long, narrow, triangular instrument, of eight or nine strings.[6] The instrument points downward. Strutt calls it a harp, but it may be simply an attempt to picture the triangular psaltery, for it is quite unlike any other drawing of the harp. Other representations of the harp may be seen on the Breac Moedog,[7] on a capital of St. Gabriel's chapel at Canterbury,[8] and in the Harleian manuscript, 603.[9]

[Eins der altenglischen rätsel, nr. 55 (Grein 56), gibt 'die harfe' zu raten auf. Dietrichs deutungen 'goldverzierter schild' und 'schwertscheide' sind unhaltbar. Daß es sich um die dreieckige harfe handelt, ergibt sich aus *wulfhēafed-trēo* v. 12. Ich habe die auflösung 'die harfe' bereits Anglia, Beiblatt V (1894), s. 50 gegeben. Wegen der einzelheiten der auslegung sieh meine demnächst in diesen Beiträgen erscheinende ausgabe der Altengl. Rätsel. Auch rätsel 27 (Grein 29) hat ein

---

[1] See Table of Old Engl. and Mod. Engl. Equivalents.
[2] See Didron, Annales Archæologia 3. —; Sullivan-O'Curry, Manners and Customs of the Ancient Irish 1 dxviii.
[3] Strutt, Horda 1 pl. 19.
[4] Westwood, Palæographia Sacra.
[5] See Table of Old. Eng. and Mod. Eng. Equivalents.
[6] Strutt, Horda 1. pl. 17.
[7] Didron, An. Arch. 5. 43, 138—140.
[8] Arch. Cantiana 13. 49.
[9] Strutt, Sports and Pastimes 176.

saiteninstrument, wahrscheinlich die harfe, zum gegenstande. Trautmann.]

The Lyre.

The use of the lyre by the Old English people is very doubtful. There is no Anglicised form of the word, and the Latin word, lira, occurs but twice, once in Ælfrics glossary, and again in a poem by Aldhelm. The poem describes the music at the dedication of a certain nunnery, and a lyre of ten strings is mentioned. The following is an extract from the poem:

'Dulcibus antiphonae pulsent accentibus aures,
Classibus et geminis psalmorum concrepet oda,
Hymnistae crebro vox articulata resultet,
Et celsum quatiat clamoso carmine culmen.
Fratres concordi laudemus voce Tonantem
Cantibus et crebris conclamet turba sororum.
Hymnos ac psalmos et responsoria festis
Congrua promamus subter testudine templi,
Psalterii melos fantes modulamine crebro,
Atque decem fidibus nitamur tendere lyram.'[1]

It is probable that Aldhelm here refers to the harp, for Ælfric, who must have been well acquainted with the poems of Aldhelm, glosses *lira* as *hearpe*.

This conclusion is strengthened by a comparison of certain illuminations. In a ninth or tenth century manuscript of Angers, David is represented as seated upon a throne, and striking, with his fingers, a five-stringed lyre.[2] This manuscript contains a series of drawings so similar to others, in mss. of approximately the same date, at St. Emeran, St. Blaise, Boulogne (the Great Latin Psalter written at the abbey of St. Bertin, while Odbert presided), and the British Museum (the Cotton. ms., Tiberius C. 6), that there can be no doubt that they are copied from each other, or from a common original. In the Cottonian ms., David is represented, in the drawing corresponding to the one just mentioned, as playing the harp.

---
[1] Migne, Patrologia Latina 89, 290.
[2] M. de Coussemaker, Annales Archaeol. 3, 82.

All of the other drawings of the lyre can be traced to Roman originals. In the Utrecht Psalter, probably of the eighth century, are representations of the classic lyre, accompanying psalms 46, 67, 70, 149. The last is reproduced in Westwood's Facsimiles,[1] and has three strings to be played with the fingers. But the Utrecht Psalter is Roman in so many respects that it is not safe to call these cuts representations of an English instrument. Strutt[2] gives a cut of a lyre of six strings from Eadwine's Canterbury Psalter of the twelfth century; this Ms., however, is copied, either directly after the Utrecht, or after another Psalter contained in the Ms. Harleian 63, which copies the Utrecht. The Tenison Prudentius,[3] and the Cleopatra C. 8,[4] which is the Psychomachia of Prudentius, a Ms. of the last of the tenth century, contain similar pictures representing a person dancing to the music of a lyre and double-pipe. The lyre has ten strings and is beaten by a baton. The value of these illuminations, however, as exponents of Old English instruments, despite the seemingly English drapery of the dancer, is impaired by the fact that a similar drawing is used with the 30 psalm, in the Utrecht Psalter, to represent the 'commorantium in circuitu', or the 'varietates supervacue'. In Tiberius B. 5,[5] which is the Astronomical Treatise of Aratus, is an eight-stringed lyre, but this manuscript also is full of Roman drawings.

The Psaltery.

Whether or not the church brought the lyre to England, it certainly brought the psaltery. The first biographer of Dunstan, the unknown 'Auctor B', who knew Dunstan well, says that he often made ten-stringed psalteries.[6] Then we have the testimony of Aldhelm, in the poem above quoted,[7] to the use of the psaltery in worship. Again, in the Spelmann and Canterbury Psalters, *psalterium* is translated invariably by *saltere*. And yet more significant, as coming from the everyday life of the people, is the superstition that a dream in which one sees cymbals or psalteries is a token of easy trading.[8]

---

[1] pl. 29.   [2] Horda 2, pl. 1.   [3] Westwood, Facsimiles.
[4] Strutt, Sports and Pastimes 176.
[5] Strutt, Horda 1. pl. 21. 8.   [6] Stubbs, Mem. of Dunst. 49.
[7] page 31.   [8] Leechdoms 3. 202. 14.

For descriptions of the psaltery we must turn to the ecclesiastical writings. The Church Fathers, as stated above, distinguish the psaltery from the cithara by the position of the resonance chamber. St. Augustine thus describes the difference between the two instruments: 'Psalterium est organum, quod quidem manibus fertur percutientis, et chordas distentas habet; sed illum locum unde sonum accipiunt chordae, illud concavum lignum quod pendet et tactum resonat, quia concipit aerem, psalterium in superiore parte habet. Cithara autem hoc genus ligni concavum et resonans in inferiore parte habet. Itaque in psalterio chordae sonum desuper accipiunt, in cithara autem chordae sonum ex inferiore parte accipiunt: hoc interest inter psalterium et citharam.'[1] The same distinction occurs five other times in the writings of St. Augustine[2], in the spurious works of St. Jerome[3], in Cassiodorus[4], in Isidore[5], in Rabanus Maurus[6], and in Pseudo-Bede[7]. St. Augustine and Isidore say that the resonance chamber was made of wood, St. Eusebius, that it was made of brass.

One form of the psaltery was square, and had ten strings: Pseudo-Jerome says: 'Est autem cum chordis decem, ... forma quadrata',[5] and Rabanus Maurus confirms this: 'Psalterium, quod Hebraice nablum, Graece autem psalterium, Latine autem laudatorium dicitur, de quo in quinquagesimo quarto psalmo dicit: "Exsurge, psalterium et cithara"; non quod in modum citharae, sed quod in modum clypei quadrati conformetur cum chordis decem.'[9] In the Boulogne and Angers manuscripts, mentioned above as belonging to a related series, David is represented as playing upon a square psaltery of ten strings, with the farther volute inturning. In the corresponding Tiberius manuscript, both volutes are inturning, and half of the strings are short. These three manuscripts contain also a different style of psaltery, with inturning volutes, larger resonance chamber, and many strings. The Tiberius manuscript represents it with straight sides, the other two, with concave sides. The Angers and Tiberius manuscripts define it as 'psalterium in modum clypei', the

---

[1] Patr. Lat. 36. 671.   [2] ibid. 36. 250, 479, 900; 37. 1036.
[3] ibid. 30. 215.   [4] ibid. 70. 15, 504.   [5] ibid. 82. 168.
[6] ibid. 111. 495.   [7] ibid. 93. 1099.   [8] ibid. 30. 215.
[9] ibid. 111. 495.

Bonner Beiträge z. Anglistik. Heft 4.

Boulogne, as 'nabulum filii Jesse apud Hebreos.'[1] M. de Coussemaker reproduces a square psaltery, with a prolonged resonance chamber, from MS. 1118 of the Royal Library at Paris.[2]

A triangular psaltery is described also. Cassiodorus[3] and Pseudo-Bede[4] report Jerome as their authority for it: 'Psalterium est, ut Hieronymus ait, in modum deltae litterae formati signi.' Notker Labeo gives the following more or less fanciful history of it: 'Sciendum est quod antiquum Psalterium instrumentum decacordum utique erat, in hac videlicet deltae literae figura multipliciter mystica.' Sed postquam illud symphoniaci quidem et ludicratores, ut quidam ait, ad suum opus traxerant, formam utique et figuram commoditati suae habilem fecerant et plures cordas annectentes et nomine barbarico Rottam appellantes, mysticam illam Trinitatis formam transmutando.'[5] Isidore calls it a 'canticum' and likens it to the harp: 'Est autem similitudo citharae barbaricae in modum Δ litterae.'[6] Rabanus questions the comparison made by Isidore: 'Est autem similitudo citharae barbaricae (ut alii volunt) in modum deltae litterae.'[7]

Gerbert reproduces a triangular psaltery,[8] and the same instrument in a reversed form, known as a cithara. MS. 1118 of the Royal Library at Paris contains a figure of a man blowing a horn, and bearing a slender triangular instrument, not unlike the harp. M. de Coussemaker, somewhat fancifully to be sure, considers it a form of the psaltery so akin to the harp that it made possible the replacement of the former by the latter.[9] In support of this supposition the last illumination mentioned under the harp should be recalled. Call it by what name we please, there was a triangular instrument which was popular for centuries.

The Sambuca and the Nabulum.

Mention should be made of these two instruments, although there is little likelihood that they actually existed in England.

---

[1] Strutt, Horda 1. pls. 20 and 21; Westwood, Facsimiles pl. 37; Ann. Arch., 3. 85.

[2] Ann. Arch. 3. 84.   [3] Patr. Lat. 70. 15.   [4] ibid. 93. 1099.

[5] Fides Sancti Athanasii Episcopi 40.   [6] Patr. Lat. 82. 168.

[7] Patr. Lat. 111. 498.

[8] De Cantu et Musica Sacra pl. 24; Ann. Arch. 3. 87.

[9] Ann. Arch. 3. 86.

To be sure, *sambucus*, defined as *saltere*, occurs in an early glossary,¹ but this definition is based upon the descriptions in the writings of the fathers, where the sambuca is alluded to only in a traditionary way.² An attempt to picture the sambuca is found in MS. Tiberius C. 6 where it is represented as an odd pear-shaped instrument of four strings.

Pseudo-Jerome,³ Cassiodorus,⁴ and Rabanus Maurus,⁵ speak of the nabulum as the Hebrew psaltery. It has been noted under psaltery, that an instrument, which in one manuscript is described as 'psalterium in modum clypei', is described in another as 'nabulum filii Jesse apud Hebreos.' In the Tiberius manuscript, and in the manuscripts at Angers and Boulogne'⁶ are semicircular instruments, rather ornate, with upper resonance chambers, and with ten or twelve strings stretched perpendicular to the base, between the base and a parallel bar. Doubtless these also are attempts to figure the instruments described by the Fathers, for there is nothing in the contemporary literature to substantiate the existence of the nabulum in the medieval period.

The Cithara.

From an early period, *cithara* was a generic name for stringed instruments. It is thus that Cassiodorus uses the word: 'Tensibilia sunt chordarum fila, sub arte religata, quae amodo plectro percussa mulcent aurium delectabiliter sensum; in quibus sunt species cithararum diversarum.'⁷ Isidore mentions several of these instruments to which this general name is applied: 'Paulatim autem plures ejus species exstiterunt, ut psalteria, lyrae, barbiti, phoenices, et pectides, et quae dicuntur indicae, et feriuntur a duobus simul. Item aliae, atque aliae, et quadrata forma, et trigonali. Antiqua autem cithara septem chordis erat.'⁸ Rabanus Maurus quotes Isidore: 'Tertia divisio rythmica pertinens ad nervos et pulsus, cui dantur species cithararum diversarum.'⁹

---

¹ Wright's Vocabularies 278. 11.
² See Isidore, Patr. Lat. 30. 214, 82. 167; Rabanus Maurus, Patr. Lat. 111. 499.
³ Patr. Lat. 30. 215.   ⁴ ibid. 70. 15.   ⁵ ibid. 111. 498.
⁶ See Strutt, Horda 1. 20; Ann. Arch. 3. 87.
⁷ Patr. Lat. 70. 1209.   ⁸ Patr. Lat. 82. 167.
⁹ Patr. Lat. 111. 496.

The classic cithara had a quadrangular or semiovoid body with hollow curving arms, and with from four to seven strings. Probably this instrument was not known in medieval times. The Great Latin Psalter at Boulogne, and MS. Tiberius C. 6 of the British Museum, the interrelation of which has been noticed before,[1] contain an instrument called the cithara. The general shape of it is that of a parallelogram, but one of the narrow ends is rounded, and the opposite end has a prolonged corner, possibly intended to rest over the shoulder. The strings, six in one manuscript, and nine in the other, are strung obliquely.[2]

If this is the style of an instrument known as the cithara, have we evidence that would show its existence in England? The word *cytere* translates *cithara* in the Vespasian Psalter, and once in the Cambridge Psalter, elsewhere *cithara* is translated invariably by *hearpe*. With the word *cithara* occuring so often in the writings of the fathers, who were studied diligently, it is not surprising that the English borrowed it. But that it did not name a distinct instrument is pretty well proved by a passage in a life of Dunstan. Auctor B. says: 'sumpsit secum ex more cytharam suam quam lingua paterna hearpam vocamus.'[3] If the cithara had been known at all, in England it would probably have been known at the court of Wessex, and if so, it would be impossible for one associated with Dunstan to confuse it with the harp.[4]

The Chorus.

The Boulogne and Tiberius manuscripts, mentioned above, contain another instrument very similar to the cithara just described; it is called a chorus.[5] In the Boulogne manuscript, the chorus has two heavy strings; in the other manuscript, it has four slender ones crowded into one corner of the open space. The following poor Latin accompanies the latter: 'Hoc est forma ejus de quatuor chordas habeth de ligno modulatus chorus est.' Nothing more is known of this instrument.[6]

[1] See p. 31.   [2] See Ann. Arch. 3. 88; Strutt, Horda 1. pl. 20.
[3] Stubbs, Mem. of Dunstan 21.
[4] See Rote, p. 41.
[5] See Ann. Arch. 3. 88; Strutt, Horda 1, pl. 20.
[6] *Chorus* was also the name of the bagpipe, see p. 51.

The Timpan, the Crwth, and the Rote.

These instruments, because of a probable interrelation, should be considered together.

How such a curious circumstance came about we cannot tell, but the word *tympanum*, which was usually applied to the tambourine, came to mean a stringed instrument in Ireland and in Scotland. Giraldus Cambrensis who wrote in the twelfth century mentions its existence: 'Hibernia quidem tantum duobus utitur et delectatur instrumentis, cythara scilicet et tympano; Scotia tribus, cithara, tympano, et choro; Gwallia vero cithara, tibiis et choro'.[1]

What was the nature of this Irish and Scotch timpan? In the Old Irish text, Agallamh na Seanorach — the Dialogue of the Ancient Men — a timpan is described whose treble strings were of silver, its pins of gold, and its bass strings of white bronze. In Cormac's description of Aengus, in the legend of the Forbais, the youth plays a wonderful timpan. The following is O'Curry's translation of the passage:

> There appeared to me upon the brow of Temair
> A splendid youth of noble mien;
> More beautiful than all beauty was his form,
> And his dress ornamented with gold.
>
> He held a silver timpan in his hand;
> Of red gold were the strings of that timpan;
> Sweeter than all music under heaven
> Were the sounds of the strings of that timpan.
>
> A wand with melody of music sweet an hundredfold;
> Over it (the Timpan [?]) were two birds;
> And the birds, no silly mode,
> Used to be playing upon it.
>
> He sat beside me in pleasant fashion;
> He played for me his delicious sweet music;
> He prophesied most powerfully then,
> That which was intoxication to my mind.[2]

---

[1] 5. 154.
[2] Sullivan-O'Curry, Manners and Customs 3. 362.

The 'wand with melody of music sweet' evidently means a bow. Further evidence that the timpan was a bowed instrument is furnished by the Brehon Laws, contained in a manuscript in Trinity College, Dublin, and quoted by O'Curry: 'The timpanist has a wand and hair.'[1] But the timpan was played also with the fingers, for in the Laws special provision is made for the timpanist who loses his nail: he was to receive, not only the usual compensation, but a 'quill nail' in addition.[2]

The timpan was not the same as the harp, for they are mentioned together frequently. Were there, then, two instruments called timpan, one played with the fingers and the other with the bow? This would hardly be reasonable, for some distinction would have been made in the Laws, where the two are mentioned together. There was one instrument, then, bearing the name timpan, whose strings were played with the fingers, or with the bow. Of course such an instrument was originally played only with the fingers, for the use of the bow invariably is a late development and may not have been known, even in the British Isles, before the eighth century. O'Curry suggests that the timpan, like the modern crwth, or crowd, may have had heavy strings for picking, in addition to the lighter strings for the bow. Let us venture another step: may not the timpan and the crwth have been the same? But we are anticipating.

The evidence pointing to a knowledge of the timpan among the Old English is satisfactory. In his biography, Osbern says of Dunstan: 'Iterum cum videret dominum regem saecularibus curis fatigatum, psallebat in tympano, sive in cithara, sive alio quolibet musici generis instrumento, quo facto tam regis quam omnium corda principum exhilarabat.'[3] This timpan was hardly a tambourine, unless the nerves of King Edmund were constituted quite differently from those of his English descendants. Further, Ælfric translates *tympanum* by *hearpe* in Exodus 15. 20, where Miriam and the women go forth with timbrels and with dances. In the Spelman Psalter, *tympanum* is translated always by *glīgbēam*, a word which

---

[1] ibid 3, 363.
[2] ibid 3, 364.
[3] Stubbs, Mem. of Dunstan 79.

elsewhere is applied to the harp,[2] and in the Thorpe Psalter, a *timpanum of ten strings* is interpolated in the sixty-seventh psalm.

Tentatively, we present as a possible illustration of the timpan of the seventh century, an instrument, unknown to Roman manuscripts, which appears in illuminations undoubtedly executed by Irishmen, in the Psalter of St. Augustine, and in the Bede Cassiodorus.[2] The instrument is oval in shape, with the sides slightly concave, furnished with five strings in one drawing, and with six in the other, the strings being played through an oval opening in the upper part of the instrument.

The Welsh crwth is first mentioned by Venantius Fortunatus, in the sixth century, where it is called the instrument of the Britons.[3] This, of course, was not a bowed instrument; had it been so, the practice of using the bow would have spread to the continent before id did, the first indication of a bowed instrument, on the continent, being in the last of the eighth or beginning of the ninth century. Subsequently, the crwth became a bowed instrument. We have cuts of it as it existed a century ago. It is an oblong box, two inches in depth, and nearly two feet in length, rounded at the bottom, and slightly tapering toward the square top. A finger-board is made possible by openings cut on either side of the centre of the upper part, and in the lower part are two sound-holes. Four strings run from a tail-piece over a flat bridge, and over this finger-board, and two other strings project beyond the finger-board. These last are touched with the thumb, the others with a bow.[4]

Hawkins gives a figure of a crwth, differing somewhat in detail. Thus one foot of the bridge enters one of the sound-holes, the other rests on the belly before the other sound-hole.[5]

Just when did the bow begin to be used with the crwth? This we cannot say, but in an eleventh-century manuscript

---

[1] See Glossary, *Gligbeam*.
[2] See Westwood, Facsimiles pls. 3, 18.
[3] See p. 29.
[4] See Ann. Arch., 3. 150; Sullivan-O'Curry, Manners and Customs I. CCCXCVI; Sandys and Forster, Hist. of the Viol. 33.
[5] Hist. of Music 2. 237; Sandys and Forster, Hist. of the Viol., 35.

of the Royal Library at Paris, is a drawing of a man playing an instrument which is probably a crwth. In general construction it is like the modern crwth, though both of the ends are rounded, and the sides are slightly inturning. It is provided with a bridge, and with three strings, which are played through are opening, as in the later crwth, and with a coarse-strung bow.[1] This instrument is not a fiddle, as has been wrongly supposed, because instruments of the fiddle order were well developed by the eleventh century.[2]

But what right have we to say that this drawing is probably a crwth? There is only one bowed instrument, with the exception of a long box entirely different in character, the relation of which to the violin style of instrument is not apparent. The eighteenth-century crwth could not have come from the fiddle which was too superior in structure and convenience to have given rise to a poor and clumsy instrument. On the other hand, the superiority of the fiddle caused it to supplant the crwth on the continent. In sequestered Wales, however, the crwth did not disappear until a century ago, for among the common people, and especially in removed districts, instruments stubbornly persist in perpetuating their forms. The ancestor of the eighteenth-century crwth, therefore, must have been remarkably like this eleventh-century instrument. Nor should we be misled by the small number of strings, for oftentimes the true number is not represented in illuminations. Moreover, the figure of a similar instrument at Worcester Cathedral has five strings.

There is sufficient evidence that the English were familiar with the crwth, from the occurence of its name in Old English. Curiously enough, it is defined by Somner as *multitudo*, a meaning that crowd did not have until the sixteenth century.

As to the relation of the timpan to the crwth. Both the Irish and the Welsh had two stringed instruments, and one of these instruments was the harp. In Ireland the word *crut* was applied to the harp, showing that both the Irish and the Welsh used the name. Then, if the Irish *crut* is the Welsh

---

[1] See Ann. Arch. 3. 151; Sandys and Forster, Hist. of the Viol. 28; Sullivan-O'Curry, Manners and Customs 1. CCCCXCVIII.

[2] See fiddle, p. 42.

telyn or harp, is the Welsh *crwth* the Irih *timpan*? It is a familiar fact in Welsh tradition, that the Irish were their schoolmasters in music. It is hardly to be supposed, then, that an instrument known to the Irish, and to the Scotch as well, according to Giraldus, should not have been known to the Welsh. Here are two nations of kindred blood, notably musical, having the harp in common, and each possessing one other stringed instrument, which is played sometimes with the bow, and sometimes with the fingers. Is there not good reason for thinking these instruments identical? But once more, among the ornaments on Melrose Cathedral in Scotland, built in 1136, was an instrument like the crwth we have pictured, yet Giraldus calls the second stringed instrument of the Scotch a timpan.

But we have one other instrument of this group to consider, or, if you will, another form of the same instrument, the *chrotta, or rotta*. Such was the name that the continent borrowed from the Welsh. The rote appears frequently in early German literatur. Otfrid mentions it with the fiddle, in the ninth century:

Sih thar ouh ál ruarit, thaz órgana fuarit,
líra joh fídula joh mánagfaltu suégala,
Hárpha joh rótta, joh thaz io gúates dohta,
thes mannes múat noh io giwúag.[1]

Notker Labeo, who speaks of the rote as a seven-stringed instrument of the minstrels, says that it was an outgrowth of the triangular psaltery, its shape being changed, that is made more oval, to suit their convenience.[2] Of course this is a fanciful supposition, but yet this passage bears good evidence to the style of the instrument.

More suggestive, in the light of certain illuminations, is a letter written in the eighth century by Cuthbert, a Northumbrian, to Lullus, a German bishop, in which he says: 'Delectat me quoque cytharistam habere, qui possit citharisare in cithara, quam nos appelamus rottae, quia citharam habeo, et artificem non habeo. Si grave non sit, et istum quoque meae dispositioni mitte. Obsecro ut hanc meam rogationem ne despicias, et risioni

---

[1] 5. 23. 197 ff.   [2] See p. 34.

non deputes.'[1] In the ninth-century manuscripts of St. Blaise and of St. Emeran, mentioned above, is an instrument called 'cithara teutonica.' The general shape of this instrument is oval, though the sides are quite deeply concave. The lower part of the instrument is solid, and in the upper part is an opening, as in the instruments described under the crwth and timpan, for playing. In one manuscript, the instrument is provided with seven strings, and in the other, with five. The stringed instruments mentioned in early German texts, so for as I have been able to discover them, are the fiddle, the psaltery, which was square or triangular, the harp, the lyre, and the rote. The term 'cithara teutonica' could hardly have been applied to the lyre, a Roman instrument; must we not conclude, then, that it refers to the rote? This conclusion is substantiated by the similarity between the shape of this instrument and that of the probable crwth, the differences being only such as would be incidental to the use of bow.

By the twelfth century *rotta* signified a bowed instrument, — though here we are getting on dangerous ground, for *rotta* came to stand for almost any stringed instrument in the later Middle Ages.[2]

To summarise then: the rote and the crwth are related etymologically, and the balance of probability favors the identity of the crwth and the timpan. We have probable drawings of the fingered form of the rote and of the bowed form of the crwth, and these drawings differ decidedly from any other representations of early instruments, with the exception of this oval instrument with the slightly concave sides, which is found in Irish illuminations, and which we have temporarily been regarding as a timpan. In these three instruments, the timpan, the crwth, and the rote, I think we have different forms of one original instrument, which the Kelts gave to England and to the Continent, and I think that these illuminations represent that instrument, subject, of course, to its vicissitudes.

The Fiddle.

The fiddle, or *fidele*, which was so popular in England from the thirteenth century, is met with but once in extant

---

[1] Patr. Lat. 96. 839.
[2] See p. 59 for a percussion instrument known as *rotta*.

Old English: Ælfric glosses it, together with the cognate *fidelere* and *fidelestre*. The earliest instance of its use is in Otfrid.[1] The earliest reproduction is from a manuscript of the eighth or ninth century. This fiddle is a pear-shaped instrument, with one string, a tail-piece, a bridge, and two semicircular sound-holes.[2] In Gori's 'Thesaurus Veterum Diptychorum' is reproduced, from a manuscript of the ninth century, a group in which one of the attendants of David plays upon a three-stringed fiddle of oval shape, furnished with a finger-board, two crescent-shaped sound-holes, a tail-piece, but with no bridge. Of a little later date is an odd fiddle in MS. Tiberius C. 6; it is a pear-shaped instrument, with four strings, two circular sound-holes placed beside the tail-piece, but with no bridge. It is performed upon with a heavy bow. To the accompaniment of this instrument a man is tossing balls and knives.[3] A Saxon Psalter, Ff. 1. 23, contains a fiddle much like the one just described. By the twelfth century we find the oval shape coming into use, and such fiddles may be seen in the drawings in the second volume of Strutt's Horda.

The Organ.

The organ as we find it in early England cannot be appreciated unless we give it its historical setting. The first organs were nothing but rude pipes bound together, or a coarse species of bagpipe. Before the time of Christ, however, hydraulic organs of rather elaborate mechanism were in use. Hero of Alexandria, in his work on pneumatics, gives detailed instruction for building such organs. Water was to be forced into a cylinder by a piston, and the air thus driven forth escaped into a box with which the pipes could be put into communication at the will of the organist. Other descriptions of hydraulic organs are furnished by Vitruvius, who lived under Caesar and Augustus,[4] and by Athenaeus, who lived in the third century.[5] We find the organ gaining early recognition

---

[1] See p. 41.
[2] See Gerbert, De Cantu et Musica Sacra pl. 32; Ann. Arch. 3. 152; Sandys and Forster, Hist. of the Viol. 51.
[3] See Strutt, Horda 1. 19; Sandys and Forster, Hist. of the Viol. 52.
[4] De Architectura 10. 11.
[5] 4. 75.

among the ecclesiastics, thus Tertullian alludes to the hydraulic organ in the following enthusiastic words: 'Specta portentosissimam Archimedis munificentiam, organum hydraulicum dico, tot membra, tot partes, tot compagines, tot itinera vocum, tot compendia sonorum, tot commercia modorum, tot acies tibiarum, et una moles erunt omnia. Sic et spiritus, qui illic de tormento aquae anhelat, non ideo separabitur in partes, quia per partes administratur, substantia quidem solidus, opera vero divisus.'[1]

By the fourth century the pneumatic organ was the more popular, and the hydraulic organ gradually went out of use. The new style of organ stood in royal favor, for the Emperor Julian is the supposed author of the following enigma:

Ἀλλοίην ὁρόω δονάκων φύσιν· ἤπου ἀπ' ἄλλης
Χαλκείης τάχα μᾶλλον ἀνεβλάστησαν ἀρούρης,
Ἄγριοι, οὐδ' ἀνέμοισιν ὑφ' ἡμετέροις δονέονται,
Ἀλλ' ἀπὸ ταυρείης προθορὼν σπήλυγγος ἀήτης,
Νέρθεν ἐϋτρήτων καλάμων ὑπὸ ῥίζαν ὁδεύει.
Καί τις ἀνὴρ ἀγέρωχος ἔχων θοὰ δάκτυλα χειρός,
Ἵσταται ἀμφαφόων κανόνας συμφράδμονας αὐλῶν·
Οἳ δ' ἁπαλὸν σκιρτῶντες, ἀποθλίβουσιν ἀοιδόν.[2]

Also on an obelisk, erected at Constantinople by the Emperor Theodosius, were carved two organs, each having seven pipes, and supplied with bellows, the operation of which necessitated the weight of two men.

The organ which Augustine describes half a century later must have been similar to these: 'Alterum ergo organum psalterium, alterum cithara. Organa dicuntur omnia instrumenta musicorum. Non solum illud organum dicitur, quod grande est, et inflatur follibus; sed quidquid aptatur ad cantilenam, et corporeum est, quo instrumento utitur qui cantat, organum dicitur.'[3]

If the testimony of Pseudo-Jerome may be trusted, the organ had attained to imposing proportions by his time, and those who doubt the accurracy of his descriptions must acknowledge that he made a most clever anticipation. The following

---

[1] Patr. Lat. 2. 669.
[2] See Du Cange.
[3] Patr. Lat. 36. 671; 37. 1964.

are his words: 'ad organum, eo quod majus esse his in sonitu, et fortitudine nimia computantur clamores, veniam. De duabus elephantorum pellibus concavum conjungitur, et per quindecim fabrorum sufflatoria comprehensatur: per duodecim cicutas aereas in sonitum nimium, quos in modum tonitrui concitat: ut per mille passuum spatia sine dubio sensibiliter utique et amplius audiatur, sicut apud Hebraeos de organis quae ab Jerusalem usque ad montem Oliveti et amplius sonitu audiuntur, comprobatur.'[1] The foregoing is found almost without change in Rabanus Maurus.[2]

A description by Cassiodorus is interesting because of its possible connection with some quaint illuminations which are found in the Utrecht and Canterbury Psalters. Cassiodorus says: 'Organum itaque est quasi turris quaedam diversis fistulis fabricata, quibus flatu follium vox copiosissima destinatur; et ut eam modulatio decora componat, linguis quibusdam ligneis ab interiore parte construitur, quas disciplinabiliter magistrorum digiti reprimentes, grandisonam efficiunt et suavissimam cantilenam.'[3] The organs in the drawings are about twelve feet in height, and have eight and ten pipes respectively. Four men are straining at the bellows, while two organists (magistri), who sit above, are scolding them. As we see the hinder side of these organs, there is nothing to indicate how the pipes are put into communication with the air chamber. These organs are presented frequently as illustrations of early English instruments, but this is absurd because of the Roman character of the Utrecht and Canterbury drawings.[4]

In 757 the Byzantine Emperor Constantine, at the urgent solicitation of Pepin, sent him a large organ, with leaden pipes.[5] In view of the fact that Pepin had to make such an exertion to procure an organ, it is surprising that we find the English familiar with large organs at least half a century earlier. Aldhelm introduces an organ with a thousand pipes into his poem 'De Laudibus Virginum':

---

[1] Patr. Lat. 30. 213.
[2] ibid 111. 496.
[3] Patr. Lat. 59. 240.
[4] See Westwood, Facsimiles pl. 29; Ann. Arch. 4. 31; Strutt, Horda 1. pl. 33.
[5] A full discussion of this transaction is in Ann. Arch. 3. 279.

Quis Psalmista pius psallebat cantibus olim,
Ac mentem magno gestit modulamine pasci,
Et cantu gracili refugit contentus adesse,
Maxima millenis auscultans organa flabris,
Mulceat auditum ventosis follibus iste,
Quamlibet auratis fulgescant caetera capsis.[1]

One would be inclined to think that Aldhelm was describing some organ which he had seen at Rome, or of which he had heard from Theodore and Hadrian, were it not that an organ of good proportions is described in the eighty-sixth riddle:

Wiht cwom gongan, ðær weras sætou
monige on mæðle mode snottre,
hæfde an eage and earan twa
and II fet, XII hund heafda,
hryeg and wombe and honda twa,
earmas and eaxle, anne sweoran
and sidan twa. Saga, hwæt ic hatte!"[2]

Dietrich comments on the riddle as follows: 'Dunkler ist nr 83 das einäugige ding mit den 1200 häuptern. dass gerade zwölf hundert, ein volksmässiges grosses tausend, genannt sind, scheint von der alliteration mit "zwei füsse" herbeigeführt, und nicht zu betonen. dem anfange "Ein wesen kam gegangen, wo manche männer im gespräch sassen" wird völlig genüge gethan wenn ein ding, etwa ein zur erheiterung der versammlung dienendes instrument getragen, also mit zwei füssen, hereinkommt, vergl. 32, 8—12. ich denke an die orgel des weltlichen gebrauchs, die schon sehr früh bekannt war, und zwar mit tausenden von pfeifen — gestützt auf Aldelmus de laud. virg. s. 138 *maxima millenis auscultans organa flabris.*'[3] I am inclined to think that a church organ is meant, the second line is more suggestive of a congregation and worship than of a social gathering, and the description tallies well with that of Aldhelm. [Was dies rätsel wirklich bedeutet, weiss ich noch immer nicht (vgl. Anglia, Beiblatt V, s. 51). Dietrich riet zuerst

---

[1] Patr. Lat. 80. 240.   [2] Wülker's text.
[3] Haupt, Zeitschrift 11. 485.

'die orgel', später 'einäugiger knoblauchhändler'!! Dass weder die weltliche noch die kirchenorgel gemeint ist, scheint mir so sicher wie dass zwei mal zwei vier ist. Näheres in meiner in diesen Beiträgen erscheinenden ausgabe der Altengl. Rätsel. Trautmann.]

The most elaborate description of an organ in Old English is found in a poem written by Wulfstan. It is dedicated to Bishop Elphege, in honor of an organ which he had placed in the church at Winchester. The verses are as follows:

Talia et auxistis hic organa, qualia usquam
    Cernuntur, gemino constabilita solo.
Bisseni supra sociantur in ordine folles,
    Inferiusque jacent quatuor atque decem.
Flatibus alternis spiracula maxima reddunt,
    Quos agitant validi septuaginta viri.
Brachia versantes multo et sudore madentes,
    Certatimque suos quique monent socios:
Viribus ut totis impellant flamina sursum,
    Et rugiat pleno capsa referta sinu:
Sola quadringentas quae sustinet ordine musas,
    Quas manus organici temperat ingenii.
Has aperit clausas, iterumque has claudit apertas.
    Exigit ut varii certa camoena soni
Considuntque duo concordi pectore fratres,
    Et regit alphabetum rector uterque suum.
Suntque quater denis occulta foramina linguis,
    Inque suo retinet ordine quaeque decem.
Huc·aliae currunt, illuc aliaeque recurrunt;
    Servantes modulis singula puncta suis.
Et feriunt jubilum septem discrimina vocum,
    Permisto lyrici carmine semitoni:
Inque modum tonitrus vox ferrea verberat aures,
    Praeter ut hunc solum nil capiat sonitum.
Concrepat in tantum sonus hinc, illincque resultans,
    Quisque manu patulas claudat ut auriculas,
Haud quaquam sufferre valens propiando rugitum,
    Quem reddunt varii concrepitando soni:
Musarumque melos auditur ubique per urbem,
    Et peragrat totam fama volans patriam.

Hoc decus ecclesiae vovit tua cura Tonanti,
Clavigeri inque sacri struxit honore Petri.[1]

Rimbault comments significiantly upon this organ: 'Although this curious description gives the idea of an instrument of large size and complicated mechanism, its construction must have been of a very primitive kind: Mr. Wackerbarth imagines that it possessed registers or stops; a key-board furnished with semitones; and a compass of three and a half octaves. Of the first position we have no proof whatever in the poem itself. Of the second all the writer says is, that it was provided with the seven sounds and the "lyric semitone", which latter clearly means the B flat. The alphabet alluded to was the handles of the rods and levers by which the instrument was played; the key-board was not yet invented. Of the third position it is clear that the compass did not exceed ten notes, "and for each note forty pipes", which makes up the number of *four hundred*. The *seventy* stout bellows-blowers must still remain a perplexing question. The brethren of Winchester were a rich and a large body, and the writer probably meant that it was the office of seventy inferior monks, at different periods, to succeed each other in this labour.'[2] The correctness of these conclusions, with the possible exception of the last, is evident.

William of Malmesbury records that Dunstan gave organs to the church at Malmesbury: 'Multa ibi largitus insignia, quorum quaedam ad hunc diem oblivionis senium potuerunt eluctari. Mirae magnitudinis signa, non quidem, ut nostra fert aetas, dulci sed incondito sono strepentia, organa quae concentu suo in festivitatibus laetitiam populo excitarent, in quorum circuitu hoc distichon litteris aeneis affixit,

Organa do sancto praesul Dunstanus Aldhelmo;
Perdat hic aeternum qui vult hinc tollere regnum.[3]

William further records of Dunstan that he introduced the organ generally into the English churches: 'Quapropter cum caeterarum tum maxime musicae dulcedine captus, instru-

---
[1] Patr. Lat. 137. 110—111.
[2] Hist. of the Organ 21.
[3] Stubbs, Mem. of Dunstan 301; Gesta Pontificum 407.

menta ejus tum ipse libenter exercere, tum at aliis exerceri dulce habere. Ipse citharam, si quando litteris vacaret, sumere, ipse dulci strepitu resonantia fila quatere. Jam vero illud instrumentum quod antiqui barbiton, nos organa dicimus, tota diffudit Anglia; ubi ut fistula sonum componat per multiforatiles tractus "pulsibus exceptas, follis vomit anxius auras". Hoc porro exercebatur non ad lenocinium voluptatum, sed ab divini amoris incitamentum, ut etiam ad litteram impleretur illud Daviticum "Laudate Dominum in psalterio et cithara; laudate Eum in chordis et organo."[1] So we see that the use of organs was well established before the Norman Conquest, and it is unquestionable that organs were used, in some of the churches, from the seventh century.

The Bagpipe.

Allied to the primitive forms of the organ was the bagpipe, which was known by various names, as *musa*, *chorus*, and *camena*.

In an Old English glossary of the eleventh century, *pipe oððe hwistle* defines *musa*. Names analogous to *pipe* are found in Old Norse, Old French, Welsh, and Irish, though none of these languages contains so early a reference to the bagpipe as this from the Old English.[2] In another early glossary *sangpipe* defines *camena*. *Camena* did not denote a musical instrument among the Romans, and it seems probable, therefore, that it came to mean an instrument through being confounded with *musa*. If this supposition is correct there were three Old English names for the bagpipe, *pipe*, *hwistle*, and *sangpipe*.

John Cotton, an Englishman of the twelfth century who wrote on music, called the *musa* the best of all instruments: 'Dicitur autem musica, ut quidam volunt, a musa, quae est instrumentum quoddam musicae decenter satis et jocunde clangens. Sed videamus qua ratione, qua auctoritate a musa traxerit nomen musica. Musa, ut diximus, instrumentum quoddam est, omnia, ut diximus, excellens instrumenta, quippe quae omnium vim atque modum in se continet, humano siquidem inflatur spiritu ut tibia, manu temperatur ut phiala, folle excitatur ut

---

[1] Gesta Pontificum 257.
[2] See Sullivan, Manners and Customs 1. CXXXII.

organa, unde et a Graeco, quod est $\mu\varepsilon\sigma\alpha$, id est media, musa dicitur, eo quod sicut in aliquo medio diversa coeunt spatia, ita et in musa multimoda conveniunt instrumenta.'[1]

Should we need further evidence of the favor in which the bagpipe was held by the early English, it is provided in the thirty-second riddle:

> Is ðes middangeard missenlicum
> wisum gewlitegad, wrættum gefrætwad.
> Ic seah sellic ðing singan on ræcede:
> wiht wæs no werum on gemonge,
> sio hæfde wæstum wundorlicran!
> Niðerweard wæs neb hyre,
> fet and folme fugele gelice:
> no hwæðre fleogan mæg ne fela gongan,
> hwæðre feðegeorn fremman onginneð
> gecoren cræftum, cyrreð geneahhe
> oft and gelome eorlum on gemonge,
> siteð æt symble, sæles bideð,
> hwonne ær heo cræft hyre cyðan mote
> werum on wonge. Ne heo ðær wiht ðigeð
> ðæs ðe him æt blisse beornas habbað,
> deor domes georn. Hio dumb wunað;
> hwæðre hyre is on fote fæger hleoðor,
> wynlicu woðgiefu. wrætlic me ðinceð,
> hu seo wiht mæge wordum lacan
> ðurh fot neoðan frætwed hyrstum!
> Hafað hyre on halse, ðonne hio hord warað
> bær beagum deall, broðor sine
> mæg mid mægne. Micel is to hycgenne
> wisum woðboran, hwæt (sio) wiht sie.[2]

[Auch diese deutung Dietrich's ist nicht richtig. Nicht der dudelsack, sondern ein saiteninstrument, ist gemeint. Ich habe Anglia Beiblatt V s. 49 die auflösung 'die fiedel' gegeben, war aber schon damals, wie ich es noch bin, im zweifel, ob nicht 'die chrotte' der zu erratende gegenstand ist. Näheres in meiner in diesen Beiträgen zu veröffentlichenden ausgabe der Altengl. Rätsel. Trautmann.]

---

[1] Patr. Lat. 150. 1395.   [2] Wülker's text.

Chorus is the usual name for the bagpipe among the church writers. It will be remembered that Giraldus called the *chorus* an instrument of Wales and Scotland. In the Boulogne and Tiberius manuscripts, which we have introduced together frequently, are drawings of the chorus,[1] which, from the fragments of Latin accompanying them, are suggested by the following from Pseudo-Jerome: 'Synagogae antiquis temporibus fuit chorus quoque simplex pellis cum duabus cicutis aereis: et per primam inspiratur, per secundam vocem emittit.'[2] These instruments are conventional, having a round body, and two pipes opposite each other. In the Tiberius manuscript is a second chorus, which has a square body, and two pipes for blowing, instead of one.[3] But the most satisfactory drawing is in another manuscript of this related group, the one at St. Blaise. Here a man is blowing on the short pipe of a round-bodied chorus, and, with the left hand, is fingering the opposite pipe, which has several holes, and which terminates in a grotesque dog's head.

One other instrument, curious in structure, should be described here, as it resembles these drawings of the chorus more than any other instrument. It is long and slender, slightly tapering, and at the broader end are three pipes. Some puzzling Latin accompanies it: 'Haec manus musica canticum est duo calami sunt de auricalco in ore sonantur omnem canticum quod in ore cantatur musicum est haec forma tubae tertie fistule in capite.' This drawing is in the Tiberius manuscript, and is reproduced by Strutt.[4]

The Pipes.

Pipe and *hwistle* were also the names of instruments of the flute order, for *tibicen* is glossed as *pipere oðð*e *hwistlere*, and *auledus* as *reodpipere*. The reed-pipe is the subject of the sixty-first riddle:

Ic wæs be sonde sæweallc neah
æt merefaroðe, minum gewunade
frumstaðole fæst; fea ænig wæs

---

[1] See Ann. Arch. 4. 38; Strutt, Horda 1. pl 21 (2).
[2] Patr. Lat. 30. 125.   [3] Strutt, Horda 1 pl. 21 (1).
[4] ibid 1. pl. 20 (7).

monna cynnes, ðæt minne ðær
on anæde card beheolde,
ac mec uhtna gehwam yð sio brune
lagufæðme beleolc. Lyt ic wende,
ðæt ic ær oððe sið æfre sceolde
ofer meodu(drinceude) muðleas sprecan,
wordum wrixlan. Ðæt is wundres dæl
on sefan searolic ðam ðe swylc ne conn,
hu mec seaxes ord and seo swiðre hond,
eorles ingeðone, and ord somod
ðingum geðydan, ðæt ic wið ðe sceolde
for unc anum twam ærendspræce
abeodan bealdlice, swa hit beorna ma
unere wordewidas widdor ne mænden.[1]

The pipe is the subject of another riddle, the ninth, but the allusions are too indefinite to give any idea of the structure of the pipe:

Ic ðurh muð sprece mongum reordum,
wrencum singe, wrixle geneahhe
heafodwoðe, hlude cirme,
healde mine wisan, hleoðre ne miðe,
eald æfensceop, eorlum bringe
blisse in burgum, ðonne ic bugendre
stefne styrme: stille on wicum
sittað nigende. Saga, hwæt ic hatte,
ðe swa scirenige sceawendwisan
hlude onhyrge, hæleðum bodige
wilcumena fela woðe minre.[2]

We have, then, no means of deciding satisfactorily whether the reed-pipe was different from the pipe or hwistle. *Auledus* and *tibicen* are not differentiated, and the *tibia* and *αὐλός* recall the classic double-pipe, which was provided with a mouth-piece, and with a vibrating-reed. Moreover, the Welsh were familiar with the double-pipe.[3] So it is probable that one of the instruments known as *pipe* was the double-pipe. Such pipes are shown in the illuminations of the

---

[1] Wülker's text. [2] Wülker's text.
[3] See p. 37.

Prudentius manuscripts, and also in those of the Harleian Psalter, but, as stated above, these illuminations received their inspiration from Latin drawings,[1] and therefore they cannot be taken as illustrative of English instruments. [Dietrich legt auch dies und das s. 51/52 angeführte rätsel falsch aus. Das 61ste habe ich Anglia Beiblatt V s. 50 als 'der runenstab', das 90ste ebenda s. 48 als 'die glocke' gedeutet. Ebensowenig kann ich die auflösung des gleich im folgenden angeführten rätsels mit 'die schalmey' zugeben. Wie ich glaube ist 'der kornhalm' gemeint. Näheres in meiner bevorstehenden ausgabe der Altengl. Rätsel. Trautmann.]

More satisfactory is the seventieth riddle, which describes the shawm, a wind instrument provided with mouthpieces:

Wiht is wrætlic ðam ðe hyre wisan ne conn,
singeð ðurh sidan; is se sweora woh
orðoneum geworht; hafað eaxle twa
scearp on gescyldrum. His gesceapo (dreogeð),
ðe swa wrætlice be wege stonde
heah and hleortorht hæleðum to nytte.[2]

Singeð durh sidan refers to the holes for fingering; *is se sweora woh orðoncum geworht*, to the fancifully carved neck and mouthpiece; *eaxle twa* to the protrusion of the body beyond the neck.

A good idea of the shawm is furnished by the following account of it in Mendel's Dictionary: 'Schalmei, ein uraltes Hirteninstrument, das zuerst aus Baumrinde, später aus Rohr und dann aus Holz gefertigt wurde. Die Hirten und noch die Kinder auf dem Lande pflegen im Frühjahr lange Streifen von frischer Baumrinde zu Röhren zusammenzuwinden, die oben eng und nach unten allmälig weiter werden; in die obere enge Oeffnung stecken sie zum Anblasen ein Röhrchen (Huppe) aus grüner, saftiger Weidenschale, das sie nach dem einen Ende zu verdünnen, indem sie mit dem Messer die äussere Schale wegnehmen. Mit etwas zusammengepressten Lippen wird dieses vorn plattgedrückte Röhrchen angeblasen und giebt nun diese

---

[1] See p. 32.   [2] Wülker's text.

angeblasene Tute einen schreienden, näselnden Tou von sich. Dieses kunstlose Hirteninstrument (*fistula pastoralis*, Hirtenpfeife) ist die ursprüngliche Schalmei und sie der Stammvater einer weitverzweigten und sehr alten Familie, nämlich der Rohrblasinstrumente.'

The Horns and the Trumpets.

The large number of words which define these instruments and their uses show how prominent they were in Old English life. Just what the differences were between the *blǣdhorn*, the *bledhorn*, the *fyhtehorn*, the *gūðhorn*, and the *trūðhorn* we cannot tell, if indeed any differences existed. The Latin does not help us, for the Old English people did not understand the difference between the various kinds of classic horns and trumpets. Thus *trūðhorn* translates *salpinx*, which was a straight trumpet like the *tuba*, and as a synonym for *sārga* translates *lituus*, which was a curved trumpet. Again, *sārga* translates *salpinx* and *tuba*, and *bīeme* translates *tuba*, *salpinx*, and *buccina*. From its etymology the *stocc* would seem to be a straight wooden trumpet, but yet in Ireland it was a curved trumpet.[1] However, *horn* and *bieme* are the generic names, and the words most frequently used.

The fifteenth riddle summarises the uses of the horn, and if the riddle may be taken as the possible history of a specific horn, it argues against the existence of many different species of the horn. The riddle is as follows:

> Ic wæs wæpenwiga: nu mec wlonc ðeceð
> geong hagostealdmon golde and sylfore,
> woum wirbogum; hwilum weras cyssað;
> hwilum ic to hilde hleoðre bonne
> wilgehleðan; hwilum wycg byreð
> mec ofer mearce, hwilum merchengest
> fereð ofer flodas frætwum beorhtne;
> hwilum mægða sum minne gefylleð
> bosm beaghroden; hwilum ic bordum sceal
> heard heafodleas behlyðed licgan;
> hwilum hongige hyrstum frætwed

---

[1] See Sullivan-O'Curry, Manners and Customs 3. 341.

wlitig on wage, ðær weras druncað;
freolic fyrdsceorp hwilum folewigan
wiege wegað: ðonne ic winde sceal
sincfag swelgan of sumes bosme;
hwilum ic gereordum rincas laðige
wlonce to wine; hwilum wraðum sceal
stefne minre forstolen hreddan,
flyman feondsceaðan. Frige, hwæt ic hatte![1]

The manuscripts are rich in drawings of the horns and trumpets. In MSS. Vespasian A. 1,[2] and Tiberius C. 6,[3] the royal psalmist is accompanied by musicians, some of whom are, blowing horns. A shepherd's horn is shown in the Great Latin Psalter at Boulogne,[4] and a warrior's horn in MS. Claudius B. 4.[5] In MS. Tiberius B. 5, which contains drawings illustrative of the seasons, is seen a horn being blown in the chase,[6] another being played at a feast,[7] and a third being blown, either to encourage the harvesters, or to call them from their work.[8] In the Benedictionale of St. Æthelwold a bird is blowing a horn beautifully wrought,[9] and on a capital in St. Gabriel's chapel a goat is playing a horn.[10]

Straight trumpets are illustrated in MSS. Vespasian A. 1,[11] Tiberius C. 6, where an attendant of David plays a trumpet resting upon a support,[12] Cleopatra C. d,[13] in the Latin Gospels of St. Gall,[14] and in one of the Prudentius manuscripts, F. 1;[15]

---

[1] Wülker's text.
[2] See Westwood, Facsimiles pl. 3; Strutt, Sports 172.
[3] See Strutt, Horda 1 pl. 19.
[4] See Westwood, Facsimiles pl. 39.
[5] See Strutt, Horda 1. 15.
[6] See Strutt, Horda 1. pl. 12; Sports, 5.
[7] See Strutt, Horda 1. pl. 10.
[8] Strutt, Horda 1. pl. 11.
[9] See Archæologia 24. 58; other horns of a later date may be seen in volume 3, pages 1, 13, 24.
[10] See Arch. Cantiana 13. 49.
[11] See Westwood, Facsimiles pl 31; Strutt Sports, 172.
[12] See Strutt, Horda 1. pl. 19.
[13] See Strutt, Horda 1. pl. 4.
[14] See Westwood, Facsimiles pl. 27.
[15] See Strutt, Horda 1. pl. 22.

curved trumpets in the Utrecht Psalter,[1] in MSS. Nero D. 4,[2] Cleopatra B. d.,[3] and Aurelius Prudentius F. 1.[4]

The Bells.

Ælfric defines *campana* as *micel belle,* and *tintinnabulum* as *litel belle.* The former were the large bells hung in towers, and the latter, the altar-bells and handbells. There is much evidence to show that tower-bells were common in England by the tenth, or by the eleventh, century. The second and seventh of the monastic signs published by Techmer imply a use of the two kinds of bells. The second reads: 'Ðus diacanes tacen is ðæt mon mid hangiendre hande do swilce he gehwæde bellan cnyllan wille'; and the seventh reads: 'Gyf ðu wæt be cyrcean tæcen wille, ðonne do ðu mid ðinum twan handum swylce ðu bellan ringe.' The latter refers, of course, to a heavy bell rung by a rope. In Malmesbury's life of Anselm a rising-bell, with a rope, is alluded to: 'Reclusis enim a dormitorio in ecclesiam omnium parietum obstaculis, vidit monachum, cujus id curae erat, a lecto egressum, funem signi tenere, quo monachos ammoneret surgere.'[5] In Thorpe's Chronica is found the following: 'Et Kiusius ad ecclesiam sancti Johannis apud Beverlacum turrim excelsam lapideam adjecit, et in ea .ii. praecipua signa posuit, ... similiter et in caeteris ecclesiis archiepiscopatus sui quae sunt trans Humbrum, scilicet apud Southwelham et apud Ston, signa ejusdem magnitudinis et soni contulit.'[6] Dunstan gave large bells to Malmesbury: 'Inter quae signa sono et modo praestantia.'[7] In 1035 Cnut gave two bells to Winchester.'[8] In the Laws of Ethelstan, framed in the middle of the tenth century, a bellhouse, on an estate, was recognized as a mark of property.[9] In the 'De Tintinno' of

---

[1] Westwood, Facsimiles pl. 29.
[2] See Westwood, Facsimiles pl. 13.
[3] See Strutt, Horda 1, pl. 5; these trumpets are heavy, and six feet in length; accompanying them is the following Latin: 'Tubae silent gladii reconduntur in vagina'.
[4] See Strutt, Horda 1. pl. 22.   [5] Gesta Pontificum 76.
[6] Cap. 7. sect. 10, in Twysden, Historiae Anglicanae Scriptores.
[7] Gesta Pontificum 407.   [8] Annales de Wintonia.
[9] See *Bellhūs.* Glossary.

Tatwine a bell is described as: 'superis suspensus in auris.'[1] With such evidence as this, there can be no doubt of the existence of the tower-bells in the late Saxon period.

But to decide upon the time when these bells were introduced into England is quite another matter. A monk of St. Gall made a bell for Charles the Great, and requested one hundred pounds of silver to use as alloy.[2] The bell must have weighed several hundred pounds. If such bells were common upon the continent, they would have been introduced into England. But it is not likely that they were common, for the largest bell in existence, of a date prior to late Saxon times, is the bell which hung in the tower of St. Cecilia at Cologne. It is a bell of the seventh century, and is about sixteen inches high.[3]

If the use of the Round Towers of Ireland could be determined, much light might be thrown upon the subject of bells. It is significant that Petrie, who has studied the problem of the towers more carefully than any other man, thinks that they held rather large bells. Indeed his evidence on this point seems convincing. He first quotes the following from a ninth century poem:

> He who commits a theft,
> It will be grievous to thee,
> If he obtains his protection
> In the house of a king or of a bell.

Then he produces, from the Brehon Laws, the following accounts of the duties of the *aistreoir* or *aistire* (hostiarius).
'*Aistreoir*, i. e. *uas aitreoir*, i. e. noble his work, when it is the bell of a *cloictheach*; or *aistreoir*, i. e. *isil aithreoir*, (i. e. humble or low his work) when it is a handbell.
'*Aistreoir*, i. e. changeable his work, i. e. to ring the bell, or use the keys; or, *uaistreoir* (high his work) when the bell is that of a *cloictheach*; or *istreoir*, i. e. low his work, when it is a handbell.' Supplementing this, he quotes from lives of

---

[1] Hook, Archbishops 1. 206.
[2] De Gestis Caroli 1. 31.
[3] See Ann. Arch. 4. 95.

St. Patrick, as follows: 'Sinell of Cill Airis, his aistiri', and 'Sinell, the man of the ringing of the bell.'[1]

Petrie is supported in his conclusion by Sullivan. The latter discusses the matter as follows: 'Open bells appear to have been in use in the Irish Church from the very first, and in early times to have afforded in certain cases a measure of the legal rights of a church. Thus for instance, a church was entitled to share the property of strangers dying within sound of its bell, and if situated on the shore of a lake or of the sea, to all "flotsam and jetsam", that is, to some such rights as are now claimed as "admirality droits". It was only the original bell, under the protection of which a *Tuath* had placed itself, that could be used for measuring the rights of jurisdiction of a church; hence, no doubt, one of the chief objects in building the Cloictigi or bell houses, known as "round towers" was to extend the area over which the sound could be heard'.[2] It seems unreasonable to suppose that simple handbells would have been rung, if these towers were to serve such purposes. However, no large Irish bells are extant, although many old square handbells are to be seen at St. Gall, and in the British Museum, and in the Museum of the Royal Irish Academy'.[3]

The handbells are referred to continually in the versions of the monastic rules. Of course the English church, in conformity with the universal custom, employed them in worship. A custom hitherto overlooked by writers upon the bell was the use of handbells at funerals. In that part of the Bayeux tapestry which pictures the funeral of Edward, four boys are shown, accompanying the body, and bearing bells. The abbot Laffetay, who has written an historical and descriptive sketch of the Tapestry, comments upon this as follows:

"Enfin", dit M. du Méril, "de chaque côté du corps, marche un enfant de chœur agitant une sonnette, et cet usage anglais semble n'avoir jamais été suivi en France". Que cet usage soit anglais, nous l'accordons volontiers; mais qu'il n'ait jamais

---

[1] Round Towers and Ancient Architecture of Ireland 381—384.
[2] Sullivan-O'Curry, Manners and Customs, 1. DXXXV.
[3] For cuts see Wilson, Prehistoric Annals of Scotland 2. 461—471; Margaret Stokes, Early Christian Art in Ireland 52—65; Westwood, Facsimiles pl. 52; Strutt, Horda 1. pl. 20; Ann. Arch. 4. 97—99; for further references see Reeves, Adamnan's Life of St. Columba 120, 187, 202.

été suivi en France, ceci est le contraire de la vérité. Pour nous en convaincre, nous n'avons pas eu besoin de pousser nos recherches au-delà de la Normandie. L'usage que l'on nous conteste y est encore suivi dans certaines paroisses des diocèses d'Évreux, de Lisieux, et de l'ancien diocèse de Bayeux. De plus, on nous l'écrit de différents côtés, cet usage est immémorial. Les confréries de charité ont à leurs gages des enfants de chœur, habillés par elles, qui accompagnent les morts au cimetière, en agitant ces clochettes.'

In the monastery at Abingdon there was a wheel which supported a number of little bells, and this instrument, which was called a rotta, was one of the cherished possessions.[1]

The Cymbalum.

In the oft-quoted manuscripts of St. Emeran and St. Blaise, there is a drawing of an instrument called a *cymbalum*. It consists of a handle and ten strings, to which are attached two rows of little bells. This instrument explains the seemingly strange translation of *cymbalum* by *belle*, in the Lambeth Psalter. Durandus speaks of a cymbalum which hung in a cloister, and which was used to call monks to the refectory,[2] and Gregory speaks of a cymbalum being struck as passing-bell.[3]

The Bombulum.

A curious instrument, called the bombulum, or bumbulum, is described by Pseudo-Jerome: 'Fistula praeterea artis esse mysticae, sicut fusores earum rerum affirmant: reperitur ita. Bombulum aereum ductile quadratum latissimumque, quasi in modum coronae cum fisoculo aereo ferreoque commixto, atque in medio concusso, quod in ligno alto spatiosoque formatum superiore capite constringitur: alterum altero capite demisso: sed terram non tangi a plerisque putatur, et per singula latera duodecim bombula aerea, duodecim fistulis in medio positis, in catena fixis dependent. Ita tria bombula in uno latere per circumitum utique figuntur, et concitato primo bombulo, et concitatis duodecim bombulorum fistulis in medio positis, clamorem

---

[1] Chronicon de Mon. Abingd. 2. 278.
[2] Rationale 1. 4. § 2.
[3] Dialogues 1. 9.

magnum fragoremque nimium supra modum simul proferunt. Bombulum itaque cum fistulis, id est, doctor in medio Ecclesiae est, cum spiritu sancto, qui loquitur in eo: constringitur in ligno alto, id est, Christo, qui a sapientibus ligno vitae comparatur: in catena, id est, in fide: et non tangit terram, id est, opera carnalia: duodecim bombula, id est, duodecim apostoli: cum fistulis, id est, divinis eloquiis.'[1]

A description, differing slightly in detail, as if trying to correct this inexplicable Latin, is found in the writings of Rabanus Maurus: 'De fistula autem refertur ita, quod sit bumbulum aereum ductile quodratum, latissimumque, in modum coronae cum fistulo aereo ferreoque commisto, quod in ligno alto speciosoque formato superiore capite constringitur. In hoc quoque per singula latera duodecim bumbula aerea duodecim fistulis in medio positis in catenis dependent; ita tria bumbula uno bilatere per circuitum utique finguntur: et concitato primo bumbulo, et concitatis duodecim bombulorum fistulis in medio positis, clamorem magnum fragoremque nimium supra modum simul proferunt. Bombulum itaque cum fistulis, id est doctor, in medio Ecclesiae est cum Spiritu sancto, qui loquitur in ea, constringitur in ligno alto, id est, in Christo, qui a sapientibus ligno vitae comparatur: in catena, id est, in fide, et non se jungit terrae, id est, operibus carnalibus. Duodecim Apostoli cum fistulis, id est, cum divinis eloquiis.'[2]

Drawings of this instrument are found in three related manuscripts of the ninth century, the St. Emeran manuscript, the Boulogne Psalter, and MS. Tiberius C. 6. From a rectangular crane is suspended, by a chain, a square ornamented box, on either side of which project arms, curving downward, and supporting, or ending in, little square boxes, or bells, ten or twelve in number. The perspective is so poor that it is impossible to tell just how the artist intended to have these supported. Several absurd explanations of the instrument have been made, notably those by Sullivan,[3] and by Mendel,[4] who having seen only the drawing from the St. Emeran manuscript, were misled by the ornamentation.

---

[1] Patr. Lat. 30. 214.
[2] Patr. Lat. 111. 497.
[3] Sullivan-O'Curry, Manners and Customs 1. d. XXXVIII.
[4] Dictionary.

However, any attempts at explaining the bombulum must prove unsatisfactory. The *bombulum aereum ductile quadratum latissimumque* is the rectangular box shown in the drawings. But what is the *fisoculo*? The word is not found elsewhere, and its etymology is uncertain. Rabanus Maurus emends it to *fistulo*, and betters the interpretation little by so doing. The *in modum coronae* doubtless means that the *fisoculo*, or *fistulo*, is a mixture of brass and iron, as in a crown. But allowing the correction by Rabanus, what is the relation of this *pipe* or *piping* to the box called *bombulum*? The explanation suggestes itself that this box is made of piping, but the box is called brazen; again, perhaps a pipe, or piece of pipe, serves as a tongue to strike the box in the interior (in medio concusso), but, so far as is known, the tongues of bells were solid, and did not resemble a pipe at all. Further, the *duodecim fistulis in medio positis* is puzzling. These may be pipes which connect the little bombula with the large bombulum, or they may be tongues which strike within the little bombula, as the large *fistulum* within the large bombulum, or they may be clappers which are suspended between the bombula, to strike them when swayed. The *concitato primo bombulo* seems to indicate an instrument of percussion, but we can say nothing more with safety. There is nothing to warrant the suggestion that this is a wind instrument. It may be that the bombulum is only an imaginary instrument. Rabanus Maurus copied the description by Pseudo-Jerome, emending it only slightly, and there is nothing that points to an acquaintance with the instrument on the part of Rabanus. Of course the monks would feel it their duty to picture the instrument, however absurd, and the bombulum is not the only instrument that suggests a fertility of imagination on the part of the monk who originated this series of drawings.

The Cymbals.

Although little reference is made to cymbals, their existence in England is probable. The sign, which made a dream of cymbals a token of easy trading,[1] shows familiarity with an instrument of this name. It may be that the *cymbalum* is

---

[1] Leechdoms 3. 202. 14.

meant, but this was a monastic instrument, and would hardly be familiar to business men. Furthermore, we have a correct description of the cymbals in Pseudo-Bede: 'Cymbala sunt ex permistis metallis minimae phialae compositae, ventricula artificiosa modulatione collisae; acutissimum sonum delectabili collatione restituunt.'[1]

The Drum.

The *tunnebotm*, by which Ælfric glosses *timpanum*, was probably a rude drum, made from the bottom of a cask. But the Old English had good drums, for in an illumination in the Saxon Psalter, Ff. 1, 23, one of the attendants of David is beating with two sticks upon a semi-spherical drum.[2]

The Rattle.

With this instrument we complete the study. We know nothing of the rattle, though we may gain something of a suggestion from the nature of the word which defines it, *cleadur*.

---

[1] Patr. Lat. 93. 1102.
[2] Westwood, Palaeog. Sacra.

Glossary.

Āblāwan: to blow the trumpet, [to blow].
 DF. 110: Nænfre mon ðæs hlude hyman *ablawed*.
Æfendrēam: vespers.
 Som.: æfensang: *æfendream*.
Æfenlēoð: an evening lay.
 Exod. 201: Forðon wæs in wicum wop up ahafen, atol *æfenleoð*
Æfenlof: vespers, see *PMLA*.
Æfensang: vespers, see *PMLA*.
Æfensceop: an evening singer, bard.
 R. 9. 5: eald *æfensceop* corlum bringe blisse in burgum.
Æfenðēowdōm: vespers, see *PMLA*.
Æftersang: matins, or lauds, see *PMLA*.
Æftersingend: the leader of the response in antiphonal singing.
 W. W. 129. 23: *æftersingend*: succentor.
Āgalan: to sing portentous music, [to ring out, sound].
 El. 27: Fyrdleoð *agol* wulf on wealde, wælrune ne mað, 342;
 B. 1521: Hringmæl *agol* grædig guðleoð; *Jul.* 615: Da cwom semninga hean hellegæst; hearmleoð *agol* earm and unlæd; *Gu.* 1320: He ða wyrd ne mað, fæges forðsið; fusleoð *agol* wineðearfende and ðæt word cwæð.

Andswarian: to respond in antiphonal singing (L. respondere).
 DCM. 627, 642: cnafan on swyðran dæle chores ða mid geswegre singan stæfne, and twegen on wynstran dæle gelice ða *andswarian*, 643, 755, 761, 762, 888; *Herr. Arch.* 24, 47, 49.

Answēge: harmonious.
 W. W. 129. 44: *answege* sang: simphonia.

Antefn: an anthem (L. antiphon).
 BR. 38. 7: sex scalmas mid *antiphonum*; 41. 1; 42. 12: se syx and syxtigoða scalm buton *antempne* forðrihte; 43. 4; 45. 6; 47. 14; 48. 1, 7; 56. 10; 79. 1, 11; 81. 1; *Gr. BR.* 33. 13; 35. 10; 39. 20; 41. 7, 10, 15; 49. 5; 71. 6; 72. 16; *DCM.* 240: singan *antefn* be rode syððan *antefn* seō be marian, 243, 358, 477, 500, 518, 519, 532, 533: To scalmum

ðæs æfenes *antefnas* beon geewedene be ðam yleau freolse, 545, 549, 550, 561: mid ðrim *antefnum* of ðære sealmsange gesettum, 569, 571, 573, 577, 623: Dær æfter cildum ongynnendum *antefnas*, 624, 639, 675, 690, 761, 766, 809: ðænne beran he singende *antefnas*, 811, 861, 874, 892, 898, 899, 905, 908, 910: Si ongunnen *antefn* on ðam godspelle, 919, 921, 926, 975; *Herr. Arch.* 19: Æfter ðysum ðam cildum ðisne *antifen* beginnendum 'Pueri Hebreorum', syn ða palmtwiga todælede, and swa ða longran *antifenas* singende gan to ðære heofodcyrican, 43; *C. Æ.* 36: ðone *antemn*, 'Vespere autem sabbati'; *Bd.* 60. 18: Da heo ferdon and nealehton to ðære ceastre, hi ðeosne letaniam and *ontemn* gehleoðre stefne sungon: 'Deprecamur te, domine, in omni misericordia tua ut auferatur furor tuus, et ira tua a civitate ista et de domo sancta tua quoniam peccavimus.

Antefnere: the antiphonary, book of anthems, (L. antiphonarium).

DCM. 571: singende antefnas se on *antefnere* synd hæfde, 634, 1014, *Herr. Arch.* 38; *Techmer* 2. 119. 3: ðonne ðu *antiphonariam* habban wille, ðonne wege ðu ðine swiðran hand and crip ðiune ðuman.

Antemn, Antemp, Antifen, Antiphon, see Antefn.

Asingan: to sing (L. decantare [d], psallere [p]), [deliver a speech].

B. 1159: Leoð wæs *asungen*, gleomannes gyd; (d) *Bd.* 242. 35: He æghwylce dæge ealne saltere on gemynde ðære godcundan herenysse *asunge*; (p) *Th. Ps.* 91. 1: God is ðæt man Drihtne geara andette, and neodlice his naman *asinge*; *Lchdm.* 2. 112, 27: *Asing* ofer nigon siðum literaria.

Āðēotan: to blow a horn, [to sound].

D.J. 109: Næfre mon ðæs hlude horn *aðyled* ne hyman ablaweð.

[Āwrecan]: to sing, [recite, utter].

B. 2108. Dær wæs gidd and gleo: hwilum hildedeor hearpan wynne, hwilum gyd *awræc* soð and sarlic.

Bēacen: 1. a signal made with a bell. 2. a bell (by metonymy)? (L. signum).

I. A signal.

Gr. BR. 67. 20: Sona swa ðæt *beacen* ðæs belhringes gehyred bið; *Gr. L.* 3. 14. 107: Deofol us lærcð slæpnesse and sent us on slæwðe, ðat we ne magon ðone beorhtan *beacen* ðære bellan gehyran; *DCM.* 404.

II. The bell?

A. Rung to mark the canonical hours.

DCM. 569: ðære sylfan on timan nihte ær ðam ðe dægred sanga *becnu* beon gestyrude, 591; *Gr. BR* 72. 14; *Herr. Arch.* 172.

B. Rung during the service.

DCM. 902: ongynne ðæne ymen; ðam ongunnenum samod beoð gehringde calle *becnu*: æfter ðæs ende cweðe se mæssepreost ðæt fers, 525, 530, 537, 853.

C. Rung during a procession.
DCM. 1117: Đanon he byð boren into eyrecan singendum callum and gestyredum callum *becnum*.

Bēamere, see Bȳmere.

Begalan: to utter enchantment.
Æ. LS. 14. 73: He genam ða ane cuppan mid ewcalmberum drence, and clypode swyðe to sweartum deoflum, and on heora naman *begol* done gramlican drence; *Lchdm*. 1. 190, 10: gyf hwyle yfeldæde man oðerne *begaleð*; 388. 14: Syge gealdor ic *begale*, sigegyrd ic me wege.

[Begiellan]: to scream.
Seaf 24: Ful oft ðæt earn *bigeal* urigfeðra.

Belhring: bell-ringing (L. sonitus campanæ).
Gr. BR. 67. 20: sona swa ðæt beacn ðæs *belhrineges* gehyred bið.

Belhūs, see Bellhūs.

Bell, see Belle.

Belle: 1. a bell (L. campana [c], clocca, tintinnabulum [t]).
2. a cymbalum, see Introduction, (L. cymbalum [cy]).
Æ. Gl. 314. 9: *belle*: clocca; 314. 10: micel *belle*: campana; litel *belle*: tintinnabulum; *Blick. Gl. belle:* cymbalum.

I. A large bell.

A. Rung to announce the canonical hours.
Æ. C. 11: Hostiarius is ðære cyrecan durewerd, se sceal mid *bellan* bicnigan ða tida; (c) DCM. 273: *bellan* gecnylledre onginnan tide ða ðriddan; Æ. Coll. 36. 1; (?) Gr. Pr. 3. 14. 107.

B. Rung as an expression of rejoicing.
SC. 261. 36: cusen ða munecces abbot of hem self and brohten him into cyrce mid processionem, sungen 'Te Deum', ringden ða *belle*.

C. Rung to call to prayer at a death.
(c) *Bd.* 340. 6: ða gehyrde heo semninga in ðære lyfte uppe cuðne sweg and hleoðor heora cluegan (Bodleian Text *bellan*) ðær heo gewunedon to gebedum gecegde and awehte beon, ðon heora hwyle of worulde geleored wæs (cf. IV. Shrn. 149. 9).

II. A little bell.

A. Used in the monastic observances.
(t) DCM. 212: Oð ðæt witodlice cildra inngan ða cyrecan an on sundron se gehringed *belle*, (t) 246: ongynnan primsang buton *bellan* tacne, (t) 393, (t) 398, (t) 724: oððæt *belle* sige cnylled; ðænne fore stæppendum embegange æfter fylige eall geferræden and callum on beodderne sittendum.

B. Worn by the priest.
(t) *G. PC.* 93. 4: Forðæm wæs beboden Moyse ðæt se sacerd scolde bion mid *bellum* behangen, (t) 12, (t) 15, (t) 95. 3, (t) 13.

III. A cymbalum.
(cy) *Lamb. Ps.* 150. 5: Heriað hine on *bellum*.

IV. Unclassified references.
Æ. H. 2. 156. 4: Ða ahcng se munune ane lytle *bellan* on ðam stanclude, 6, 10; *CD.* 4. 275: Ðær næron ær buton, vii. upphangene *bella*, and nu ða synd .xiii. upphangene; *Shrn.* 149. 9: Seo ylce godes ðeowen gehyrde on ða ylcan tyd ða heo gewat wundorlice *bellan* sweg on ðære lyfte; *Techmer* 2. 118. 7: swilce he gehwæde *bellan* cnyllan wille, 16: Das cyricweardes tacen his ðæt mon sette his twegen fingras on his twa eagan and do mid his handa, swylce he wille ane hangigende *bellan* teon, 18; *L. Eth.* 6. 501; *L. Edg.* 8: Hryðeres *belle* bið anes scill weorð.

Bellhūs: a bell-house.
W. W. 327. 16: *belhus* cloccarium.
LR. 2: Gif ceorl geðeah ðæt he hæfde fullice fif hida agenes landes, cirican and cycenan, *bellhus*, and burhgeatsetl, and sundernote on cynges healle, ðonne wæs he ðonouforð ðegenrihtes weorðe.

Belltācen: a signal made with a bell.
Gr. Pr. 3. 11. 65: Sona swa hy ðæt *belltacen* gehyrað ðære nigoðan tide, ðæt is seo nontid.

Bēme, see Bīeme.

Bemere, see Bymere.

Bēodfers: a hymn sung at meal time.
Gr. Dial. 1. 19 *beodfers*: ad mensam, carmen, hymnus.

Beorhtm: music, [noise, clang, cry, revelry].
Hall.

Bergelsong: a funeral song or dirge.
Leo 116: byrgensang (*bergelsong*): grabgesang.

Besingan: to enchant, [to bewail].

I. To enchant.
Æ. H. 1. 476. 9: he sceal nan man mid galdre wyrte *besingan*, ac mid Godes wordum hi gebletsian, and swa ðiegan; *Lchdm.* 1. 202. 13: Wið næddran slite, genim ðas ylcan wyrte, ðe we ebulum nemdun, and ær ðam ðe ðu hy forceorfe heald hy on ðinre handa and cweð ðriwa nigon siðan, 'Omnes malas bestias canto', ðæt ys ðonne on ure geðeode, *besing* and ofercum ealle yfele wilddeor.

II. [To bewail].
Gu. 587: ge deaðe sceolon weallende wean wope *besingan*.

Bīeme: a trumpet.
Hpt. Gl. 423. 9: *byman*: classicæ; 467. 4: *bymum*, 1 here: classibus; 525. 19: *byman*: salpicis; *Blick. Gl. beme*: tuba; *W. W.* 360. 19: *beme*: barbita; *Corpus Gl.* 571: *beme*: concha, 2015: *beeme*: thessera.

I. Used as a signal.
  A. In war.
   El. 109: *Byman* sungon hlude for hergum; *B.* 2943: Frofor eft gelamp sarigmodum somod ærdæge, syððan hie Hygelaces horn and *byman* gealdor ongeaton, ða se goda com leoda dugoðe on last faran; *Exod.* 159; *Æ. H.* 2. 212. 39; *Æ. LS.* 25. 352.
  B. In camp.
   Exod. 216: Moyses bebead eorlas on uhttid ærnum *bemum* folc somnigean, frecan arisan, 132: Bræddon æfter beorgum, siððan *byme* sang, flotan feldhusum, 222; *Ep. Alex.* 252: Da het ic blawan mine *byman* and ða fyrd faran, 293, 388.
  C. In heralding a king.
   Shrn. 95. 13; swa swa *byme* clypeð beforan cyninge.
  D. For worship.
   Dan. 179: Da wearð hæleða hlyst, ða hleoðor cwom *byman* stefne ofer burhware. Da hie for þam cumble on cneowum sæton, onhnigon to ðam herige hæðne ðeode, 192.
  E. At the Judgment Day.
   Chr. 882: Ðonne from feowerum foldan sceatum ðam ytemestum corðan rices englas ælbeorhte on efen blawað *byman* on brehtme, 1062; *DJ.* 51; *Sat.* 602; *BH.* 95. 13; *Æ. H.* 1. 616. 4, 10, 11; 2. 568. 23 (2); *Eccl. Inst.* 467. 4; *Ph.* 497; *Shrn.* 82. 22.
  F. On Sinai.
   Æ. H. 1. 312. 12; 2. 196. 24: Dær begann to brastligenne micel ðunor, and liget sceotan on ðæs folces gesihðe, and *byman* bleowan mid swiðlicum dreame, and micel wolcn oferwreah calne ðone munt; 202. 23, 29.

II. Used in joyful music.
   Zu. Ap. 32. 17: ðar wearð ormæte blis, and ða organa wæron getogene and ða *biman* geblawene; *Sat.* 172, 238; *Ph.* 134: Ne magon ðam breahtme *byman* ne hornas, ne hearpan hlyn ne ænig ðara dreama, ðe dryhten gescop gumum to gliwe in ðas geomran woruld.

III. Metaphorically used.
   D.J. 110; *BH.* 163. 21; he wæs *beme* Cristes, fricca on ðysne middangeard, 32; *Æ. H.* 1. 456. 23: His stemn is swylce ormæte *byme*; *G. PC.* 91. 20.

IV. In translation from the Scriptures.
   Tuba: *Judg.* 7. 16; *V. Ps.* 46. 6; *C. Ps.* 46. 6; 80. 4; 97. 6 (2); 150. 3; *Spel. Ps.* 46. 5; 80. 3; 97. 6 (2); 150. 3; *Th. Ps.* 46. 5; *Lamb. Ps.* 80. 4; *Skt. Mt.* 6. 2; *Lind. Mt.* 6. 2; *Rush. Mt.* 6. 2; 24. 31. Buccina: *Ex.* 19. 13, 16, 19; 20. 18; *Josh.* 6. 4, 12; *Judg.* 7. 19.

Birisang: a funeral song or dirge.
>Hpt. Gl. 458. 3: wopleoð 1 *birisang* 1 licsang: tragoediam (gl. miseriam, luctum).

Blǣdhorn: a horn.
>W. W. 142. 33: *blœdhornas*: classica.

Blǣshorn: a horn:
>L. Edg. 8: Hryðeres belle, and hundes hoppe, and *blœshorn*; ðissa ðreora ælc bið anes scill weorð, and ælc is melda geteald.

Blāwan: to blow the trumpet or the horn, [to breathe].
>Æ. Gr. 137. 5: ic *blawe*: flo.
>Æ. H. 1. 312. 12: Dær com micel leoht, and egeslic sweg, and *blawende* byman; 2. 196. 24; 212. 31: On ðam seofoðan dæge swiðlice *bleowan* seofon sacerdas mid sylfrenum bymum; BH. 95. 13; SC. 258. 23; Zu. Ap. 32. 17; Sat. 602; Chr. 881.
>In translation from the Scriptures.
>Clangere: Ex. 19. 13; Josh. 6. 4, 12, 16; Judg. 7. 19. Insonare: Judg. 3. 27. Buccinare: Spl. Ps. 80. 3.

Blāwung: the blowing of trumpets, [blast].
>Judg. 7. 16: Da het Gedeon his geferan habtan heora byman him mid to ðære *blawunge*.

Bleðhorn: a forest-horn.
>CD. 3. 362. 22: renne scolforhammenne *bleðhorn*.

Bletsingsealm: the Benedicite.
>Gr. BR. 36. 18: æfter ðisum ðone *bletsingsealm*, ðæt is 'Benedicite'.

Blissesang: a song of joy (L. laetitiae canticum).
>Bd. 264. 27: Da geherde he eft ðone ileau *blissesong* upp oð heofonas mid unasecgendre swetnesse oft hweorfan; Chad. 111.

Brȳdlēoð: a marriage song.
>Hpt. Gl. 481. 13: *brydleoðes*: epithalamii (gl. triclinii).

Brȳdsang: a marriage song.
>W. W. 129. 24: *brydsang*: ymencus, vel epithalamium.

Bȳme, see **bīeme.**

Bȳmere: a trumpeter.
>Æ. Gr. 40. 7: *bymere*: tubicen; Æ. Gl. 302, 5: *bymere*: tubicen; W. W. 190. 8: *bymere*: salpista, aule; 279. 6: *bemere*: tubicen; 480. 5: *bemeras*: tubicines.
>Lind. Mt. 9. 23: gecwom ðe hælan in hus aldormonnes and geseah *beameres*.

Bȳmesangere: a trumpeter.
>W. W. 190. 9: *bymesangere*: salpica.

Bȳmian: to blow the trumpet.
>W. W. 190. 10: ic *byme*: salpizo, vel buccino.
>Lamb. Ps. 80. 4: (L. Buccinate tuba).

Byrgensang: a funeral song or dirge.
Leo 116: *byrgensang* (bergelsong): grabgesang.
Cantere: a singer, leader of the church music (L. cantor).
DCM. 904: Fram *cantere* sona beo ongunnan antefn mid sealm.
Cantic: 1. a canticle or exalted portion of Scripture set to music for church use. 2. a song. (L. canticum).
I. A canticle.
BR. 41. 4, 5; 43. 16; 44. 1; 45. 15; 51. 1; *Gr. BR.* 35. 13: æfter ðæm ðry *canticas* of witigena bocum swylce se abbod gesette, and ða syn mid alleluian begunnene; 38. 2: *cantic* deuteronomio, ðæt is 'Adtende celum', se sy todæled on twegen glorian, 4: Elles oðrum dagum on ðære wucan sy *cantic* gesungen, ðæt is lofsang, ðe to ðam dæge belimpð, ealswa hit romana ecclesia hylt, ðæt is on monandæge 'Confitebor', on tiwesdæg 'Ego dixi', on wodnesdæg 'Exultairt', on ðunresdæg 'Cantemus', on frigedæg 'Domine audivi', on sætresdæg 'Adtende celum'; 38. 11; 39. 18; 44. 3, 20; *DCM.* 998; *St. Gu.* 15, 13; *BH.* 5. 8; 7. 2; (used synonomously with 'Pater Noster' in the following references): *Sal.* 33, 47, 99: ForÐon hafaÐ se *cantic* ofer ealle Cristes bec widmærost word.

II. A song, found in the following Scriptural translations.
Deut. 31. 19, (c) 22: Moises wrat ðone *cantic* and lærde Israela folc; *Spl. Ps.* 32. 3; 39. 4; 41. 11; 136. 4; *Th. Ps.* 143. 10.

Cantor: a singer, leader of the church music.
C. Æ. 36: ac betwux ðam ðe higan to husle onginne se *cantor*, 'Alleluia', and ðone sealm ðærto 'Laudate Dominum omnes gentes', syððan ðone antemn 'Vespere antem Sabbati' and 'Magnificat' oð ende; *CD.* 4. 261: and ðer coman munkes of Ealden mynstre, ðæt wæs Ealdwig, and Wlstan *cantor*.

Ceargealdor: a sad song of enchantment.
Jul. 618: Da ewom semninga hean hellegæst, bearmleoð agol; cleopade ða for corðre *ceargealdra* full.

Chōr: 1. a church choir. 2. the part of the church occupied by the choir. 3. a choral dance. (L. chorus.)
Æ. Gr. 28. 18: *chor*: chorus; *W. W.* 546. 43: *chor*: chorus.

I. A church choir.
DCM. 278: Ðær æfter mæssan ærne mergenlice wyrðian, to ðære on oðrum dæge se swiðra offrige *chor*, se wynstra to heah mæssan, 640: Cnafan on swyðran dæle *chores* ða mid geswegre singan stæfne, 644; andswarige edemes eall *chor*, 645: ðæunenchst cild swiðran *chores* edlæccan ða ufran, 646, 680, 769, 798, 891, 944, 1053, 1054, 1131; *Herr. Arch.* 49.

II. The part of the church occupied by the choir.
(?) *BR.* 76. 5; (?) 78, 16; (?) 105. 5; (?) *Gr. BR.* 68. 9; (?) 70. 13; (?) 115. 4; *DCM.* 369: Syððan gan to serydenne hi ða ðenas ge-

scrydde soðlice inngan to *chore*, 699: Ealle gebroðru *chor* inngan, 922: ongean cyrrende *chor* oððe gebedhus ðæt him gedafenlic byð geðuht to gan. *Herr. Arch.* 145: Se profost ðone secaft fram *chore* eft to *chore* bere.

III. A choral dance.

G. PC. 347. 6: on ðæm *chore* beoð manige menn gegadrode anes hwæt to singanne anum wordum and anre stefne.

In translation from the Scriptures.

Chorus: *Spl. Ps.* (M) 149. 3; *G. PC.* 347. 4.

Chōrglēo: a choral dance (L. chorus).

Lamb. Ps. 149. 3 Herian hie naman his on *chorgleowe*.

Cimbal: 1. a cymbal. 2. a cymbalum, see Introduction.

W. W. 328. 31: *cimbal*: cymbalum.

I. A cymbal.

Lchdm. 3. 202. 14: *cymbalan* oððe psalteras oððe strengas ætrinan saca hit getaenað.

In translation from the Scriptures.

L. Cymbalum: *V. Ps.* 150. 5 (2); *C. Ps.* 150. 5 (2); *Spl. Ps.* 150. 5 (2).

II. A cymbalum.

Herr. Arch. 179: swa seo *cimbalum* (L. tintinnabulum) sy geslægen, gan hi calle to beoderne; *Gr. Dial.* 1. 9.

Ciricbelle: a hand-bell.

Lchdm. 2. 136. 29; 137. 6: ðonne drince ðone drene of *ciricbellan*.

Ciricsang: the ecclesiastical music (L. carmen ecclesiasticum).

Bd. 150. 29; 208. 23; 466. 16: Eac swylce he sumne æðelne cyricsangere begeat, se wæs Mafa haten, se wæs on Cent on sangereft gelæred fram æfterfyligendum ðara discipula ðæs eadigan papan Set. Gregorii,: and he gewæðer ge ða *cyricsangas* lærde, ðe hi ær ne cuðan, ge eac, ða ðe he in cuðan and mid langre gymeleasnesse caldian ongunnon, ða eft mid his lare on ðone ærran steall geedniwode wæron.

Ciricsangere: one who taught the ecclesiastical music and led the singing during service (L. cantator ecclesiæ).

Bd. 466. 16: see *Ciricsang*.

Cītere, see Cȳtere.

Cleadur: a rattle.

Som.: *cleadur*: crepitaculum.

Clipol: the clapper of a bell.

Hall.

Clipur: the clapper of a bell.

Wanl, Cat. 109. 2. 16—20: Se bend ðe se *clipur* ys mid gewriðen, ys swylce hyt sy sum gemetegung ðæt ðære tungan *clipur* mæge

styrian, and ða lippan æthwega beatan. Soðlice mid ðæs rapes
æthrine se bend styriað ðone *clipur*.

Clugge: a bell (L. campana).

Bd. 340.6: Da gehyrde heo semninga in ðære lyfte uppe cuðne
sweg and hleoðor heora *clucgan* ðær heo gewunedon to gebedum
geeegde and awehte beon, ðon heora hwyle of worulde geleored wæs.

Cnyll: the knell of a bell (L. signum).
Sounded to announce the canonical hours.

Æ. Coll. 101.26: Daða *cnyll* ic gehyrde, ic aras of minon bedde,
and eode to cyrcean; 35.15; *BR.* §2.11,13.

Cnyllan: to knell, sound a bell (L. pulsare).

DCM. 219, 247, 273, 370, 374: Si *cnylled* ðæt forme taen nates
and si gedon gebed, 475, 591 (2); *BR.* 82.13; *Herr. Arch.* 172;
Techmer 2.118.7: Ðæs diacanes taeen is ðæt mon mid hangiendre
hande do, swilce he gehwæde bellan *cnyllan* wille.

Cruð: a crwth, see Introduction.

? Cwēman: to serve by singing.

Th. Ps. 105.11: him lofsangum lustum *cwemdan* (L. cantaverunt
laudes ejus); 107.1: Gearu is min heorte, ðæt ic Gode *cweme*,
sealmas singe soðum Drihtne (L. paratum cor meum; cantabo, et
psalmum dicam Domino).

? Cwide: a song (L. canticum), [speech].

C. Ps. 136.3: Singæð us be ðæm *cwidum* syon.

Cwidegiedd: a minstrel's lay to be sung or recited, [a speech].

Wand. 55: Fleotendra ferð no ðær fela bringeð cuðra *cwidegiedda*.

Cȳtere: a cithara.

In translation from the Scriptures.

Cithara: *V. Ps.* 32.2 Ondettað dryhtne in *citra*; 42.4; 56.9; 70.22;
80.3; 91.4; 97.5; 107.3; 146.7; 150.3; *Spl. Ps.* (C) 56.11: Aris
saltere and *cytere*.

Dægrēdsang: matins, see *PMLA*.

Drēam: 1. music, modulation, melody, harmony. 2. a chorus.
3. pleasant sound of the trumpet. 4. a musical instrument.
[ecstasy, rejoicing.]

W. W. 213.17: efenhleoðrung, vel *dream*: concentus, i. adunationes multarum vocem; 342.39: *dream*, swinsunge: armonia; *New
Ald. Gl.* 136: *dream*: armonia; 138 *dreames*: jubilationis; *Hpt. Gl.*
429.18: *dreames*: psalmodiae; 438.18: wynsumme swinsunge 1 *dream*
melodiam; 467.21: *dreame*, mid gedremere swinsunge 1 mid hleoðringendum *dreame*: consona (gl. concordi) vocis harmonia (gl. modulatione, sono); 478.18: *dreamas*: harmonias (gl. sonos, melodias);
514.1: *dream*: concentum, melodiam; 515.10: swinn, *dream*: melodiam
519.17: *dreamas*: concentus; *Som.*: dryme: *dream*.

I. Music, modulation, melody, harmony, sound.
A. Of mortals.
BR. 50. 6: æfensanc dæghwamlice mid feower sealmorum mid dreame (L. modulatione) si gesungen; Gr. BR. 43. 8; Gr. Pr. 3. 9. 384: and he heredon ða god mid swiðlicre blisse on sange and on dreame; W. H. 148. 3.
B. Of heavenly beings.
Æ. H. 2. 334. 12, 29: Hi ða sungon and seo sawul ne mihte undergitan hu heo on ðone lichaman eft becom, for ðæs dreames wynsumnysse; 342. 10; (?) 354. 4; 548. 12: Stodon twa heofenlice werod ætforan ðære cytan dura, singende heofenlicne sang, and hi tocneowen ðæt werbades men ongunnon symle ðone dream, and wifhades men him sungon ongean, andswariende; Æ. LS. 15. 212; Hi sungon ðisne sang, mid singalum dreame, Sanctus, sanctus, sanctus, dominus deus omnipotens; Gr. Pr. 3. 3. 466, (?) 480; Sat. 44, 328; Gu. 1290: engla ðreatas sigeleoð sungon; sweg was on lyfte gehyred under heofonum, haligra dream; Hy. 5. 2.
C. Unclassified.
Ph. 137: Ne magon ðam breahtme byman ne hornas, ne hearpan hlyn ne hæleða stefn ænges on corðan ne organan, swegleoðres geswin ne swanes feðre, ne ænig ðara dreama, ðe dryhten gescop gumum to gliwe in ðas geomran worold.

II. A choir.
A. Of mortals.
Dan. 258: Bliðe wæron eorlas Ebrea, ofestum heredon drihten on dreame.
B. Of angels.
Hy. 9. 36: ealle ðe heriað, halige dreamas clænre stefne; Æ. H. 2. 352. 15: ic ðær wynsume stemne ormætes dreames gehyrde; Gr. Pr. 3. 3. 481: Wynsum is seo wunung on ðam wuldorfullum dreame swa manegra ðusenda mid micclum swege; (?) An. 874: heredon on behðu halgan stefne dryhtna dryhten: dream wæs on hyhte; (?) Exod. 546.

III. The sound of the trumpet.
Æ. H. 2. 86. 35; 196. 24: Byman bleowan mid swiðlicum dreame; 202. 23: Dær wæs bymena dream hlude swegende.

IV. In translation from the Scriptures and hymns.
Organum: Spl. Ps. 136. 2; Lamb. Ps. 136. 2; ASH. 103. 7. Canor: ASH. 58. 2; 30. 12. Modulus: ASH. 103. 5.

Drēamcræft: the art of music (L. musica).
Bt. 54. 31: Gedeð se dreamcræft ðæt se mon bið dreamere; Shrn. 152. 13: musica ðæt ys dreamcræft.

Drēamere: a musician (L. musicus).
Bt. 54. 31: see Dreamcræft.

Drēamlic: musical, [joyous.]
> *W. W.* 445. 28: ðā *dreamlican*: musica; 492. 37: ðā *dreamlican*: musica.

Drēamness: singing (L. cantio).
> *Lamb. Ps.* 136. 3: word *dreamnessa* ōððe sanga (L. cantio).

Drēamswinsung (?): melody.
> *BT.*

Drēman: to make sacred music with song or with an instrument, [to rejoice].
In translation from the Scriptures.
> *Psallere: C. Ps.* 20. 14; *Spl. Ps.* 20. 13; *Lamb. Ps.* 46. 7; 97. 5. *Jubilare: Spl. Ps.* 80. 1; *Lamb. Ps.* 97. 7.

Drēme: melodious.
> *Hpt. Gl.* 467. 4: mid *dremere* stefne: canora voce.

[Dryhtlēoð]: a noble and patriotic lay.
> *El.* 342: Be ðām Dauid cyning *dryhtleoð* agol, frod fyrnweota and ðæt word geewæð wigona baldor: 'Ic frumða god fore secawode, sigora dryhten; he on geshyðe wæs mægena wealdend, min on ða swiðran ðrymmes hyrde: ðanon ic ne wende æfre to aldre onsion mine'.

Drȳman, see Drēman.

Drȳme: a song.
> *Som.: dryme:* dream.

Drȳme, adj., see Drēme.

Eǣrpung, see Hearpung.

? Ealuscop: an ale-house bard.
> *C. Edg.* 5S: We lǣrað, ðæt ænig preost ne beo *ealuscop*.

Efenhlēoðor: concord of voices, harmony.
> *Ph.* 621: Bliðe bletsiað bregu selestan, eadge mid englum, *efenhleoðre* ðus.

Efenhlēoðrung: concord of voices.
> *W. W.* 213. 37: *efenhleoðrung*, vel dream: concentus, i. aduuationes multarum vocum.

Fæt: mechanical translation of the L. 'vas' in the expression 'in vasis psalmi'.
> *V. Ps.* 70. 22: in *featum* salma; *C. Ps.* 70. 22: *Spl. Ps.* 70. 24.

[Fers]: the 'verse' of the Liturgy (L. versus).
> *Gr. BR.* 35. 7: Singe man ǣrest six scalmas and ðonne on ende *fers*; 11: Singan oðre syx scalmas mid ðrim antefnum and *fers* æfter ðam. See *BR., Gr. BR., DCM., Herr. Arch.,* for further instances.

[Fitt]: a song (L. cantilena, carmen), poem.
> *Bt.* 106. 29: Da se Wisdom ða ðas *fitte* asungen hæfde; *Met.* (introduction) 17; *Andr. Rune Pass.*

[Fittan]: to sing.

Whale 1: Nu ic *fitte* gen ymb fisca cynn wille woðcræfte wordum cyðan ðurh modgemynd bi ðam miclan hwale.

Fiðele: a fiddle.

Som.: *fiðele*: fidicula.

Fiðelere: a fiddler.

Æ. Gr. 40. 7: *fiðelere*: fidicen; *Æ. Gl.* 302. 6: *fiðelere*: fidicen; *Som.*: *fiðelere*: fidicen, pandurarius, lyricen.

Fiðelestre: a female fiddler.

Æ. Gl. 302. 6: *fiðelestre*: fidicina.

Foresingend: the leader of the singing in the church services.

W. W. 129. 21: *foresingend*: præcentor.

? Fūslēoð: a death lay.

An. 1549: Dær wæs yðfynde innan burgum geomorgidd wrecen gehðo mænan, forht ferð manig, *fusleoð* galen; *Gu.* 1320: He ða wyrd ne mað, fæges forðsið, *fusleoð* agol wineðearfende, and ðæt word acuseð; *Chr.* 623: Ic ðec ofer eorðan geworhte, on ðære ðu sealt yrmðum lifgan, *fusleoð* galan.

Fyhtehorn: a fighting- or battle-horn.

Th. Ps. 74. 9: Ealra fyrenfulra *fyhtehornas* ic bealdlice gebrece sniome (L. Omnia cornua peccatorum confringam).

? Fyrdlēoð: a war-song.

El. 27: *fyrdleoð* agol wulf on wealde, wælrune ne mað; *Exod.* 577: weras wuldres sang, wif on oðrum folcsweota mæst *fyrdleoð* golan aclum stefnum eallwundra fela.

Galan: to sing (L. cancre[e], incantare[i]), [utter, sound forth, cry, scream]. (Most of the references are given, but the extent to which they are musical is doubtful.)

I. Applied to human utterance.

A. Of joy or woe.

Exod. 577: Weras wuldres sang, wif on oðrum, folcsweota mæst fyrdleoð *golan* aclum stefnum eallwundra fela; *Rood* 67: sorhleoð *galan*; *Chr.* 623: fusleoð *galan*; *B.* 786: gryreleoð *galan*, 2460: sorhleoð *gæleð*; *El.* 124 sigeleoð *galen*; *An.* 1127: hearmleoð *galan*, 1342, hearmleoð *galan*, 1549: fusleoð *galen*; *Jul.* 629 hearm *galan*, (c) *Met.* 7. 2: He gliowordum *gol* gyd æt spelle.

B. Of incantation.

R. 21. 35: Heo firenað mec wordum, ungod *gæleð*; *Rim. P.* 24: Ic galdorwordum *gol*; (i) *Lamb. Ps.* 57. 26: Seo ne gehereð stemne *galendra*, and atterwyrhtan *galendes* wislice; (i) *C. Ps.* 57. 6; (i) *Lamb. Ps.* 57. 6; (i) *Spl. Ps.* 57. 5; (i) *Th. Ps.* 57. 4.

II. Applied to the songs or cries of birds.
El. 52: herge to hilde: hrefen uppe *gol* wan and wælcfel; *Emb.*
22: Ðu gehyrde *galan* geac on bearwe.
III. Applied to the trumpet's sound.
B. 1432: Hie bearhtm ongeaton, guðhorn *galan.*

[Galdor]: a magic song, incantation, [enchantment, divination, sorcery].
Hpt. Gl. 510. 11: *galdra*: incantationum; 519. 8: ibid.; *W. W.*
198. 23: *galdra*: cantionum.
Lchdm. 1. 388. 14: Syge *gealdor* ic begale; 2. 112. 5: Sing ðriwa ðæs halgan See Iohannes gebed and *gealdor*; 28: Asing ofer nigon siðum letania, and pater noster and ðis *gealdor* 'Acræ ærcræ ærnem nadre ærcuna hel' etc.; 322. 6: Wið lið wærce sing .viiii. siðum ðis *gealdor* ðæron and ðin spatl spiw on, 'Malignus obligavit, angelus curavit dominus salvavit'; 350. 28; 352. 5; 3. 10. 16, 17; 24. 25; 38. 3, 5; 42. 7, 17, 18; *Æ. H.* 1. 476. 8.

Galdorlēoð: a magic song, [charm, spell].
W. W. 509. 17: *galdorleðum*: carminibus.

Gearobrygd: deft playing (of the harp).
Gifts of Men 50: Sum mid hondum mæg hearpan gretan, ah he gleobeames *gearobrygda* list.

Gedd(-), see Gidd(-).

Gedrēme: harmonious, melodious, [joyous].
Hpt. Gl. 519. 17: *gedremere* swinsunge, marg. gedremum sauge: consona melodia; *W. W.* 228. 40: mid *gedremum* swege: eque sonore.
Æ. H. 1. 38. 7: Hi calle samod mid *gedremum* sange Godes wuldor hleoðrodon; 600. 9: on *gedremum* sange; *Herr. Arch.* 46: mid gedremum swege singan hludre stefne; 87, (?) 101, 105: nihtsang sy cae mid *gedremum* swege (L. æque sonore) gesungen; *ASH.* 2. 14; 115. 15: Wuldor fæder *gedrymum* (L. melodis) uton swegan mid stefnum; *Exod.* 79.

Gedrēmed: modulated.
Prud. Gl.

Gehlēoð: harmonious.
Bd. 60. 18: Hi ðysne letanian and antefn *gehleoðre* (L. consona) stæfne sungan.

Gēomorgid(d): a sad lay.
B. 3150: Hignm unrote modceare mændon mondryhtnes cwealm, swylce *giomorgyd* lat on meowle; *An.* 1548: Ðær wæs yðfynde innan burgum *geomorgidd* wreccn.

Gesingan: to sing [compose poetry].
Men. 70: Sculan we hwæðere gyt martira gemynd ma areccan, wrecan wordum forð, wisse *gesingan*; *BH.* 45. 31: mæssan *gesingan*; 207. 5.

In translation from the Scriptures.
> *Lind. Lk.* 7.32: We *gesungon* iub mid hwistlum (L. Cantavimus vobis tibiis).

Geswēge: harmonious, sonorous.
> *New Ald. Gl.* 135: of *geswegum*: consona, 187 *geswegre*: canora; *W. W.* 210.11: *geswege*: consona. *DCM.* 641: ða mid *geswegre* singan stæfne (L. sonora voce); *Æ. LS.* 7.44.

Geswin(s): melody.
> *Ph.* 137: Ne magon ðam breahtme byman ne hornas, ne hearpan hlyn ne hæleða stefn ænges on corðan ne organan, sweglcoðres *geswin* ne swanes feðre, ne ænig ðara dreama, ðe dryhten gescop gumum to gliwe in ðas geomran woruld.

Getēon: to string a musical instrument, to play an instrument, [to draw together].
> *Th. Ps.* 91.3: Ic on tyn strengum *getogen* hæfde, hu ic ðe on psalterio singan mihte; 143.10: mid tyn strengum *getogen* hearpe; *Zu. Ap.* 32.17: Da organa wæron *getogene*.

Geðwǣre: harmonious, concordant, [united, peaceful].
> *W. W.* 129.43: *geðwære* sang: armonia.

[Gid(d)]: a song, [poem, ballad, proverb, tale, saying].
I. A gleeman's song.
> *Scop.* 139: Swa scriðende gesceapum hweorfað gleomen gumena geond grunda fela, ... *gydda* gleawne; *Gn. V.* 167: gerised gleomen *gied*; *B.* 1065: Ðær wæs sang and sweg samod ætgædere fore Healfdenes hildewisan, gomenwudu greted, *gid* oft wrecen, ðonne healgamen Hroðgares scop æfter medobence mænan scolde, 1160: Leoð wæs asungen, gleomannes *gyd*, 2108, 2154, 151; *Seaf.* 1.

II. A dirge.
> *B.* 2446: ðonne he *gyd* wrece, sarigne sang, ðonne his sunu hangað hrefne to hroðre and he him helpan ne mæg.

[Giddian]: to sing, [utter in impassioned language, recite].
> *Ph.* 571: Dus frod guma on fyrndagum *gieddade* gleawmod, godes spelboda.

[Gidding]: a lay, [saying, prophecy, poetry, poetical recitation].
> *Wond. Cre.* 12: Ðæt geara iu gliwes cræfte mid *gieddingum* guman oft wrecan.

Giftlēoð: a nuptial song.
> *W. W.* 165.33: *giftleoð*: epithalamium.

Gīomorgyd, see **Gēomorgidd**.
Glēo(w), see **Glīg**.
Glēowian: to play on an instrument, [be merry, sing].
> *Spl. Ps.* 67.27: on middele mædena *glywiendra* (L. tympanistriarum).

[*Bt.* 36. 6: Ꝥa ongan se wisdom *gliowian*; *C. Edg.* 58: ꝥæt ænig preost ne *gliwige.*]

Glēoword: a song.
Met. 7. 3: *gliowordum* gol.

Glīewmēden: a gleemaiden.
C. Ps. 67. 26: Forecomon cældermæn togeðiedde singendum on midle gingra *gliewmedene* l plegiendra mid timpanan (L. timpanistriarum.)

Glīg: glee music, music that causes joy (L. musica), [glee, mirth].
Gn. V. 172: Ꝥy læs ðe him con leoða worn, oððe mid hondum con hearpan gretan, hafað him his *gliwes* giefe; *Wond. Cre.* 11: Ꝥæt geara in *gliwes* cræfte mid gieddingum guman oft wreccan; *G. PC.* 153. 25: Ꝥonne gefeng Dauid his hearpan, and gestillde his wodðraga mid ðæm *glige*; (?) *Ph.* 139: ne ænig ðara dreama, ðe dryhten gescop gumum to *gliwe*; *B.* 2105: Ꝥær wæs gidd and *gleo*.

In translation from the Scriptures.
Th. Ps. 67. 24: *gleowe* sungon (L. psallentibus).

Glīgbēam: 1. a harp. 2. an Irish timpan.
B. 2263: Nis hearpan wyn, gomen *gleobeames*; *Gifts of Men* 50: Sum mid hondum mæg hearpan gretan, ah he *gleobeames* gearobrygda list; *Chr.* 670.

In translations from the Scriptures.
Tympanum *Spl. Ps.* 80. 2; 149. 3; 150. 4; *Blick. Gl.*

Glīgcræft: the art of the minstrel.
Gr. Dial. 1. 9: *gligcræft*: ars musica, histrionia, mimica, gesticulatio.

Glīgmann: a minstrel, glee-singer. [jester, player, buffoon].
Som.: *gligman*: fidicen, tibicen tympanista.
B. 1160: Leoð wæs asungen, *gleomannes* gyd; *Gn. V.* 167: Wera gehwylcum wislicu word gerisað, *gleomen* gied; *Scop.* 136: swa scriðende gesceapum hweorfað *gleomen* gumena geond grunda fela.

Glīowian, see Glēowian.

Glīoword, see Glēoword.

Glīw, see Glīg.

Glīwhlēoðriend: a minstrel, glee singer.
B. T.

Glīwhlēoðriendlic: musical.
W. W. 446. 36: ða *gliwhleoðriendlican*: musica.

[**Glīwstæf**]: melody.
Wand. 52: ðonne maga gemynd mod geondhweorfeð, greteð *gliwstafum*, georne geondsceawað.

Glȳwian, see Glēowian.

Gomenwudu: a wooden musical instrument, a harp.

B. 1065: Dær wæs sang and sweg samod ætgærde fore Healfdenes hildewisan, *gomenwudu* greted; *B.* 2108: Hildedeor hearpan wynne, *gomenwudu* grette.

Graðul(ā?): a gradual, antiphon.

DCM. 1019: [Alleluia] for *graðulum* (L. pro gradualibus) byð gesungen.

Grētan: to play the harp, [greet, handle].

B. 1065; Dær wæs sang and sweg, gomenwudu *greted*, 2108: He gomenwudu greted; *Gifts of Men* 49: Sum mid hondum mæg hearpan gretan; *Gn. V.* 171; *Wand.* 52; *Chr.* 670.

? Gryrelēoð: a horrible lay.

B. 786: Norðdenum stod atelic egesa anra gehwylcum, ðara ðe of wealle wop gehyrdon, *gryrcleoð* galan godes andsacan, sigeleasne sang, sar wanigean hellehæfton; *By.* 285: Bærst bordes lærig and seo byrne sang *gryreleoða* sum.

Gūðhorn: a war-horn.

B. 1432: Hie onweg hruron bitere and gebolgne, bearhtm ongeaton, *guðhorn* galan.

? Gūðlēoð: a war-lay.

B. 1522: Mægenræs forgeaf hildebille, hond swenge ne ofteah, ðæt hire on hafelan hringmæl agol grædig *guðleoð*.

Gyd(d), see Gidd.

Handbelle: a handbell.

CD. 4. 275: Nu ða synd .xiii. upphangene, and .xii. *handbelle*.

Hēahsangere: the precentor, leader of church music.

Bd. 314. 3: se arwyrða wer Iohannes, Sc̄e Petre cirican ðæs apostolis *heahsongere*.

? Hearmlēoð: a song of grief.

Jul. 615: Da cwom semninga hean hellegæst; *hearmleoð* agol; *An.* 1127: Da se geonga ongann geomran stefne gehæfted for herige *hearmleoð* galan, 1342.

Hearpanstala: the neck of a harp.

W. W. 203. 36: *hearpanstala*: ceminigi.

Hearpanstapas: the neck of a harp.

W. W. 203. 7: *hearpanstapas*: ceriminglus.

Hearpe: 1. a harp. 2. a cithara.

Æ. Gl. 302. 5: *hearpe*: lira l cithara.

Seaf. 44: Ne bið him to *hearpan* hyge se ðe on lagu fundað; *Fates of Men* 80: Sum sceal mid *hearpan* æt his hlafordes fotum sittan, feoh ðicgan and a snellice snere wræstan, lætan scralletan scearo se ðe hleapeð nægl neomegende; bið him neod micel; *B.* 89, 2107, 2262: ne mæg byrnan hring æfter wigfruman wide feran

hæleðum be healfe, his *hearpan* wyn, gomen gleobeames, ne god
hafoc geond sæl swingeð ne se swifta mearh burhstede beateð, 2458,
3023: nalles *hearpan* sweg wigend weccean; *Scop.* 105: Donne wit
Scilling sciran reorde for uncrum sigedryhtne song ahofan, hlude
bi *hearpan* hleoðor swinsade; *Gifts of Men* 49; *Gn. V.* 171: Longað
ðonne ðy læs ðe him con leoða worn oððe mid hondum con *hearpan*
gretan, hafað him his gliwes giefe, ðe him god sealde; *Ph.* 135;
Gen. 1079; *G. PC.* 175. 6; 183. 25; *Bd.* 342. 22, 23; *Lchdm.* 3. 202. 15:
Hearpan gesihð orsorhnesse ccapes hit ge[taenað]; *Zu. Ap.* 27. 10—13:
'Leofe dohtor, hat feccan ðine *hearpan*, and geeig ðe to ðine
frynd and afirsa fram ðam iungan his sarnesse'. Da eode heo ut
and het feccan hire *hearpan* and, sona swa heo hearpian ongan, heo
mid winsumum sange gemægnde ðære *hearpan* sweg; 27. 19, 22, 24,
29, 31; *W. II.* 46. 16: *hearpe* and pipe and mistlice gliggamen dremað
eow on beorsele. *Rim. P.* 27.

In translation from the Scriptures.
Psalterium: *V. Ps.* 32. 2; 56. 9; 80. 3; 91. 4; 107. 3; 143. 9; 149. 3;
150. 3; *Th. Ps.* 32. 2; 143. 10. Cithara: *C. Ps.* 42. 4; 56. 9; 70. 22;
80. 3; 91. 4; 97. 5(2); 107. 3; 146. 7; 150. 3; *Spl. Ps.* 32. 2; 42. 5;
56. 11; 70. 24; 80. 2; 91. 3; 97. 6; 107. 2; 146. 7; 150. 3; *Th. Ps.* 32. 2;
42. 5; 56. 10; 70. 20; 91. 3; 107. 2; 146. 7; *Genesis* 31. 27. Tympanum: *Ex.* 15. 20, 21. Tibia: *Skt. Lk.* 7. 32.

Hearpenægl: a plectrum.
W. W. 157. 27: *hearpnægel*: plectrum.
Zu. Ap. 27. 28: Apollonius his *hearpenægl* genam, and he ða hearpe-
strengas mid cræfte astirian ongan.

Hearpere: a harper.
Æ. Gl. 302. 4: *hearpere*: citharista 1 citharoedus; *Æ. Gr.* 21. 14:
ðes *hearpere*: hic citharista; *Leiden Gl.* 147: *harperi*: fidicen.
G. PC. 175. 7: ða se *hearpere* suiðe ungelice tiehð and styreð;
Bt. 166. 29: An *hearpere* wæs on ðære ðeode ðe Thracia hatte ðæs
nama wæs Orfens; 166. 30, 33; 168. 4, 5, 11, 20; *Genesis* 4. 21: ðe wæs
fæder *herpera* (L. canentium cithara); *Genesis* (Chase) 4. 21.

Hearpestre: a female harper.
W. W. 190. 6: *hearpestre*: citharistrio.

Hearpestreng: a harpstring.
Zu. Ap. 27. 28: He ða *hearpestrengas* mid cræfte astirian ongan.

Hearpian: to play the harp.
Æ. Gr. 235. 5: fægere he *hearpað*: pulcre citharizat.
Zu. Ap. 27. 12: Da eode heo ut and het feccan hire hearpan and
sona swa heo *hearpian* ongan; *Bt.* 166. 32: Da ongann monn secgan
be ðam hearpere ðæt he mihte *hearpian* ðæt se wuda wagode;
168. 8; 170. 5(2).

Hearpsang: a psalm, song to the harp.
W. W. 129. 40: *hearpsang*: psalmus, 41: psalm æfter *hærpansang*:
canticum, 42: ær *hærpansang*: psalmus.

Hearpslege: 1. a plectrum. 2. playing of the harp.
Napier Gl. 64: *hearpslege*: plectro.
Lamb. Ps. 97. 5: on hearpan and on *hearpslege* (L. in cithara, in cithara).

Hearpswēg: the sound of the harp.
Blick. Gl. sealmleoð and *hearpsweg*: psalterium et cythara.

Hearpung: harping.
Bt. 168. 18, 33; 170. 8: Uton agifan ðæm esne his wif, forðam he hi hæfð gecarnod mid his *hearpunga*.
C. Ps. 32. 2: Ondettæð drihtne on *cærpungum* (L. in cythara).

Heofonbȳme: a heavenly trumpet.
Chr. 949: Weorpeð geond sidne grund hlud gehyred *heofonbyman* stefn.

Herebȳme: a war trumpet.
Exod. 99: Da ic on morgen gefrægn modes rofan hebban *herebyman* hludan stefnum wuldres woman.

(?) Herian: to sing praises.
ASH. 15. 5 (L. canentium); 50. 3: Fram ðære sunnanupspringes anginne oð corðan gemære criste uton *herigan* (canamus). *Th. Ps.* 7. 17; 9. 2, 11; 29. 3; 32. 2, 3; 46. 6: Ac singað urum Gode, and *heriað* hine; singað, singað, and *heriað* urne Cyning; singað, and *heriað* hine (Psallite Deo nostro, psallite; psallite Regi nostro, psallite).

Herpere, see Hearpere.

? Hildeleōð: a war-lay.
Judith 211: Ac him fleah on last earn ætes georn, urigfeðera, salowigpada saug *hildeleoð*.

Hlēoðor: melody, music, tone, [voice, sound, noise].
Scop. 105: for uncrum sigedryhtne song ahofan, hlude bi hearpan *hleoðor* swinsade; *Gu.* 1297: heofonlic *hleoðor* and se halga song gehyred wæs; *R.* 32, 17: Hwæðre hyre is on fote fæger *hleoðor*; *Ph.* 12: Dær bið oft open eadgum togeanes onhliden *hleoðra* wyn, heofonrices duru, ? 131: Bið ðæs *hleoðres* sweg eallum songcræftum swetra; *An.* 723: stefnum nerigað, halgum *hleoðrum* heofoncyninges ðrym; [The cries of birds.]
R. 25. 5: Ic onhyrge ðone haswan earn, guðfugles *hleoðor*; *Seaf.* 20: Dyde ic me to gomene ganotes *hleoðor*.
In translation from the Scriptures.
Sonus: *Th. Ps.* 107. 2: on *hleoðre* hearpan; 150. 3: *hleoðre* beman.

(?) Hlēoðorewide: song, [speech, audible utterance].
Hy. S. 2: Wutan wuldrian weorada dryhten halgan *hlioðorewidum*.

Hlēoðrian: to sing melodiously or harmoniously (L. concinere [c], concrepare [cp]), [to speak proclaim, resound].
Hpt. Gl. 467. 21: dreame, mid gedremere swinsunge ł mid *hleoðringendum* dreame: consona (gl. concordi) vocis harmonia (gl. mo-

dulatione, sono); 498. 8: *leoðrade*: concreparet (gl. resonaret), cf. the context; 519. 17: concrepantes: *hleoðriende*, see the context.

(?) *Ph.* 539: Donne *hleoðriað* halge gæstas, sawla soðfæste song ahebbað: (?) *Æ. H.* 1. 38. 7: Ili calle samod mid gedremum sauge Godes wuldor *hleoðrodon*; (?) (c) *ASH.* 2. 13; (?) (c) 14. 14; (?) (c) 29. 16: ðæt we ðe tida nyhta nu *hleoðriyende* we tobrycað; (?) (cp) 115. 1: Mid gewilnungu stefne we singað wrixlicnde *hleoðriende*.

Hlyn(n): sound of the harp.

Gen. 1080: Se ðurh gleawne gedanc herbuendra hearpan ærest handum sinum *hlyn* awehte; *Ph.* 135; *B.* 611.

Hlȳrian: to blow the trumpet (L. buccinare).

Lamb. Ps. 80. 4: Bymað l *hlyriað* mid byman.

Horn: a horn.

Æ. Gr. 80. 2: ðes *horn*: hoc cornu; 13: ðes *horn*: his cornus; 90. 6: *hornas*: cornua; *Æ. Gl.* 302. 7: *horn*: cornu; *Napier Gl.* 66: *horn*: salpix.

I. Used in military life.

B. 1423: *Horn* stundum song fuslic fyrdleoð, 2943: Frofor eft gelamp sarigmodum somod ærdæge, syððan hie Hygelaces *horn* and byman gealdor ongeaton, ða se goda com leoda dugoðe on last faran; *Exod.* 192: Wæron ingemen calle ætgædere cyningas on corðre: cuð oft gebad *horn* on heape, to hwæs hægstealdmen, guððreat gumena gearwe bæron.

II. Used in private life.

Ph. 134: Ne magon ðam breahtme byman ne *hornas*, ne hearpan hlyn ne hæleða stefn... ne ænig ðara dreama, ðe dryhten gescop gumum to gliwe; *SC.* 258. 23: Ða munceos herdon ða *horn* blawen ðæt hi blewen on nihtes; *L. Wih.* 28: Gif feorrancumen man oððe frændce buton wege gange and he ðonne nawðer ne hryme ne he *horn* ne blawe for ðeof he bið to profianne; *L. Ine* 20; *DJ.* 109.

III. In translation from the Scriptures.

Buccina: *Judg.* 3. 27. Tuba: *V. Ps.* 80. 4; 97. 6(2); 150. 3; *Lamb. Ps.* 97. 6. Cornea: *C. Ps.* 97. 6; *Spl. Ps.* 97. 6.

Hornblāwere: a horn-blower, trumpeter.

Æ. Gr. 40. 6: ðes *hornblawere*: hic cornicen; *Æ. Gl.* 302. 7: *hornblawere*: cornicen; *Corpus Gl.* 454: *hornblauuere*: cercacus; *W. W.* 364. 4: *hornblawere*: ceriacus.

SC. 258. 26: Dær mihte wel ben abuton twenti oðer ðritti *hornblaweres*.

Hornbora: a horn-bearer, trumpeter.

W. W. 263. 10: *hornbora*: cornicen; 370. 7: *hornbora*: cornicem. *El.* 54: Werod wæs on tyhte, hleowon *hornboran*, hreopan friccan: mearh moldan træd, mægen samnode cafe to cease.

Hringan: to ring a bell (L. pulsare).
  SC. 261. 36: Hi ringden ða belle; Chart. Th. 437. 13; DCM. 212, 272, 382, 524, 530, 592, 853, 902; Gr. BR. 72. 11; Herr. Arch. 131: sy non gehringed 162; Techmer 2. 118. 18: Do ðu mid ðinum twan handum, swylce ðu bellan ringe.

Humen, see Ymen.

Hwistle: a reed instrument, pipe.
  Æ. Gl. 302. 6: pipe oððe hwistle: musa; 302. 7: hwistle: fistula; W. W. 268. 20: wistle: avena; 352. 22: wistle: avena; 406. 23: wistle: fistula; 519. 15: wistle: fistula.
  Lind. Lk. 7. 32: We gesungen inh mid hwistlu (L. tibia).

Hwistlere: a piper.
  Æ. Gr. 40. 8: pipere oððe hwistlere: tibicen.
  Skt. Mt. 9. 23: Da he geseah hwistleras (L. tibicines).

Hwistlung: 1. music of the pipe. 2. songs or cries of birds.
  Lind. Lk. 15. 25: gehcrde hwistlung (L. symphonia) and ðone song; St. Gu. 48. 5: mislice fugela hwistlunge.

Hylsong: a timbrel.
  C. Ps. Hergæð hine on hylsongæ (L. tympano).

Hymen(-), see Ymen(-).

Imen, see Ymen.

Lācan: to play a musical instrument.
  R. 32. 19: Hie dumb wunað hwæðre hire is on fote fæger hleoðor; wrætlic me ðinceð hu seo wiht mage wordum lacan ðurh fot neoðan.

Lānesang: the song for the offertory.
  W. W. 130. 2: lanesang: offertorium, see note.

? Lēoð: a song, [lay, poem].
  Hpt. Gl. 438. 19: sigorlic leoð: carmen triumphale; 502. 13: sarlic-leoð: tragoedium.
  Gr. Pr. 3. 11. 120: ðæt man idele leoð ne singe on ðysum dagum; Æ. LS. 36. 540: ða deoflican leoð to singanne ðe ic ær on worulde geleornode; Gifts of Men 52: sum leoða gleaw; Gn. V. 170: Longað ðonne ðy læs ðe him con leoða worn, oððe mid hondum con hearpan gretan; Bd. 342. 5; Lchdm. 3. 10. 11, 13; Shrn. 121. 7: Se wæs ærest sumes kaseres mima, ðæt is leasere, and sang beforan him scandlicu leoð.

  In translation from the Scriptures.
  Carmen: Spl. Ps. 39. 4; Deut. 31. 19. Canticum: Deut. 31. 21.

[Lēoðcræftig]: skilled in song.
  Deor 40: Ahte ic fela wintra folgað tilne, holdne hlaford, oð ðæt Heorrenda nu, leoðcræftig monn, londryht geðah ðæt me eorla hleo ær gesealde.

[**Lēoðgidding**]: a song, [lay, poem].
   An. 1479: Hwæt! ic hwile nu haliges lare, *leoðgiddinga* lof ðæs he worhte, wordum wemde, wyrd undryme.
Lēoðian: to sing, [to resound].
   Rim. P. 40: foldan ic freoðode, folcum ic *leoðode*.
Lēoðrian, see **Hlēoðrian**.
[**Lēoðsang**]: song, [poetry].
   Bd. 344. 25: Da rehton heo him and sægdon sum halig spell and godcundre lare word: bebudon him ða, gif he meahte, ðæt he in swinsunge *leoðsonges* ðæt gehwyrfde.
Letania: a litany (L. letania).
   Bd. 60. 18: ðeosne *letaniam* and ontemn gehleoðre stefne sungon: Deprecamur te, Domine, in omni misericordia tua ut auferatur furor tuus, et ira tua a civitate ista et de domo sancta tua quoniam peccavimus; *Lchdm.* 2. 112. 27: Wið fleogendum atre and ælcum æternum swile, on frigedæge aðwer bnteran ðe sic gemolcen of anes bleos nytne oððe hinde, and ne sic wið wætre gemenged; asing ofer nigon siðum *letania*, and nigon siðum pater noster, and nigon siðum, ðis gealdor, Acrie, ærcræ etc.; 138. 17; 346. 5, 12, 19; 356. 7; 3. 12. 9. 24. 23; 62. 21. See *singan* 1. A. 9 for further references.
Lewisplega: a rowing song for keeping time.
   W. W. 202. 31: *lewisplega*: ccreuma, vel celeuma, idem et toma, i. leta cantatio.
Līclēoð: a funeral song or dirge.
   Hpt. Gl. 427. 2: *licleoð*: carmen funebre (gl. lacrimabile).
Līcsang: a funeral song or dirge.
   Hpt. Gl. 427. 2: *licsang*: epicedion (gl. carmen super cadaver); 488. 3: wopleoð l birisang l *licsang*: tragoediam (gl. miseriam luctum).
Lof: a song of praise, hymn, [praise, glory].
I. Hymn.
   BR. 42. 15; 44. 4: æfter ðisum filian *lofu* (L. laudes), see *Gr. BR.* lofscalm, 'Laudate dominum de celis'.
II. In translation from the Scriptures.
   Psalmus: *Th. Ps.* 26. 17. Hymnus: *Th. Ps.* 64. 14.
Lofsang, 1. a hymn (L. hymnus [h]). 2. a canticle (L. canticum [c]). 3. a psalm. 4. matins or lauds (L. matutinum [m], matutinalis laus [ml], laus [l]). 5. a song of praise.
   W. W. 129. 29: *lofsang*: ymnus; 235. 17: herigend sang, vel *lofsang*: fausta adclamantes, i. alto canendo.
I. A hymn or hymn-singing, the doxology.
   (h) *BR.* 41. 10; (h) 47. 6, (h) 12; (h) 48. 8, (h) 13; (h) 50. 2; *Gr. BR.* 35. 19: Beginne se abbod ðæne *lofsang* 'Te deum laudamus'; *Æ. II.* 1. 54. 27: Ure gastlican lac sind ure gebedu, and *lofsang*, and huselhalgung; 150. 29; 214. 9; 218. 4; (?) 326. 11: We wurðiað ðæs

Halgan Gastes tocyme mid *lofsangum* seofon dagas; 384. 17; 446. 26; 468. 35: Witodlice æfter ðisum com se broðor mid his folce, and ðone halgan lichaman mid wulderfullum *lofsangum* aweg ferodon; 548. 1: We sceolon on ðyssere mærlican freolstide mid halgum gebedum and *lofsangum* us geinnian, swa hwæt swa we on oðrum freolsdagum calles geares ymbrynes hwonlicor gefyldon; 600. 25; 2. 86. 10: Nu on ðære gelicnysse forlætað Godes ðeowas ða heofonlican *lofsangas*, 'Alleluian' and 'Gloria in excelsis Deo', on ðissere Septuagesima; 88. 3; 96. 31; 204. 1: ac ðillice ne magon singan.ðone *lofsang*, 'Des is se dæg ðe Drihten worhte; 412. 16: On ðisnm dæge we wurðiað on urum *lofsangum* ðone mæran Apostol Jacobum; 584. 2; *BH.* 193. 17; 201. 26; 207. 29; *Æ. LS.* 21. 165, 230, 233, 236, 246, 259; 27. 1; 28. 82; 29. 296; (?)*SC.* 156. 18: Hi ealle mid myeelan ðrymme and blisse and *lofsange* ðone halgan arcebiscop into Cantware byri feredon; *Gr. Pr.* 3. 3. 32, 37; 4. 29, 40; 6. 121; *Gifts of Men* 92: Sum cræft hafað cirenytta fela, mæg on *lofsongum* lifes waldend hlude hergan, hafað healice beorhte stefne; *Jul.* 689: Ungelice wæs læded *lofsongum* lic haligre micel mægne to moldgræfe; *Shrn.* 32. 10; 49. 22: he gesette ærest ðæt man sang 'Gloria in excelsis deo' ðone *lofsang* foran to mæssan; *Bd.* 284. 12. *Byhrt.* 320. 6: Da æðelan munceas ðære tide lof mid kyrriole and engla *lofsange* (Gloria in excelsis Deo) gewurðiað.

II. A canticle.

(c) *BR.* 42. 17; (c) 48. 3; (c) 52. 3; *Gr. BR.* 36. 21: *lofsang* of ðam godspelle, ðæt is 'Benedictus dominus deus Israhel'; 38. 4; 41. 11: *lofsang* of ðam godspelle, ðæt is 'Magnificat'; *Æ. H.* 1. 202. 25: Da sang Maria ðærrihte ðone *lofsang* ðe we singað on Godes cyrcan, æt ælcum æfensange, 'Magnificat anima mea Dominum', 28; 204. 25; 600. 9.

III. A psalm.

Æ. LS. 11. 89: Æfre we wæron gefultumode on ælcum gefeohte swa oft swa we sungon ðisne ænne sealm; 'Deus in nomine tuo salvum me fac et in virtute tua libera me'. Hi wurdon ða gelædde mid ðysum *lofsange* to ðam reðum.

IV. Lauds.

(m) *BR.* 42. 9: on mergenlicum *lofsangum*; (m) 44. 7; (m) 45. 16; (m) 46. 4; (m) 47. 2; (ml) *Æ. Coll.* 101. 29: Ic sang uhtsang æfter ða we sungon dægredlice *lofsanges*; (l) *DCM.* 238, (ml) 243, (l) 245, (l) 471; *Souls Ad.* 69: Est sona fram ðe hweorfan on hanered ðonne halige men lifiendum gode *lofsang* doð; *Æ. LS.* 21. 172; *BH.* 207. 36.

V. Songs of praise, praise-singing.

A. Songs of mortals.

Æ. H. 2. 22. 7: We sceolon eac Cristes acennednysse and his gebyrdtide mid gastlicere blisse wurðian, and us mid Godes *lofsangum* gebysgian; 160. 19: Sum munuc wæs unstæððig on Godes *lofsangum* and ne mihte his tidsangas gestandan mid his gebroðrum, ac eode him ut worigende; *Æ. LS.* 25. 505: Æfter ðysum dædum hi ðan-

codon drihtne mid *lofsangum* and andetnyssum eallra ðæra mærða
ðe he ðam iudeiscum gedyde foroft; *W. II.* 237. 20; *Gr. Pr.* 3. 9. 396:
Judith ða herode ðone heofonlican god swyðe mid *lofsange*, swa
swa hit on læden us sægð; *Bd.* 284. 12; *Shrn.* 127. 11.

B. Songs of heavenly beings.

Æ. H. 1. 90. 3: Hi standað ætforan his ðrymsetle, and singað
ðone niwan *lofsang*; 406. 4; 440. 34; 442. 7, 10. 32; 582. 31: Hi ðisne
lofsang mid micclum dreame gesungen, 'Gloria in excelsis deo, and
in terra pax hominibus bone voluntatis'; 2. 98. 4: ne gehyre ge hu
myrige *lofsangas* swegað on heofonum; *W. H.* 249. 26: Donne under-
foð ða englas ða eadigan sawle mid myclum *lofsange* and hig ge-
bringað to ecre blisse; *Gr. Pr.* 3. 3. 461; 2. 119.

VI. In translation from the Scriptures and hymns.
Hymnus: *C. Ps.* 64. 2, 14; *Th. Ps.* 39. 1; 99. 3; *Spl. Ps.* 64. 2, 14;
118. 171; *Skt. Mt.* 26. 30; *ASH.* 2. 12; 7. 19; 33. 4; 40. 7; 45. 1; 69. 3;
87. 1, 2; 108. 6; 137. 10; 139. 16; 140. 12; 141. 3, 19; 144. 4; 146. 5.
Canticum: *Th. Ps.* 53. 1; 68. 31; *Spl. Ps.* 68. 35; 95. 1; 97. 1; 136. 5;
149. 1; *Genesis* 31. 27; *Col.* 3. 16 (*Æ. H.* 1. 606. 21); *ASH.* 26. 3; 29. 7;
40. 3; 73. 16. Laus: *Th. Ps.* 105. 10. Carmen: *Ex.* 15. 1. Chorus:
Ex. 15. 21.

Lofsealm: the 148th Psalm.
Gr. BR. 36. 18: æfter ðon ðone *lofsealm*, ðæt is 'Laudate dominum de celis'.

Lofsingende: a singer of hymns.
Hpt. Gl. 519. 17: *lofsingende*: hymnizantes.

Mæssesang: the celebration of the mass.
W. H. 171. 6; 173. 21; and mæssepreosta gehwylc do, swa hit
micel ðearf is, on his *mæssesancgum* clipje to Criste; 245. 7; *CD.*
4. 276; *Shrn.* 81. 20; 84. 3; 88. 3; 119. 2. *Eccl. Inst.* 471.

Magister sanges: a teacher of ecclesiastical music (L. magister
ecclesiasticae cantionis).
Bd. 258. 26: Ond ærest buton Jacobe ðæm songere bi ðæm we
beforan her sægdon, wæs *songes magister* Norðanhymbra ciriccan
Ædde haten.

Middægsang: sext, see *PMLA*.

Midsingend: one who assists the leader of the singing in the
church services.
W. W. 129. 25 *midsingend*: concentor.

Mirigness: melody, [mirth].
W. W. 33. 31: *myrgnis*: musica; *Corpus Gl.* 1352: *myrgnis*: musica.

Mōtbell: a bell rung to call to a moot.
Schmid 509 § 4: Debent statim pulsatis campanis, quod Anglice
vocant *motbel*, convocare omnes et universos, quod Anglice dicunt
folcmote.

Nægl: a plectrum.
> *Fates of Men* 84: see next word.

Nēomian: to sound melodiously.
> *Fates of Men* 84: Sum sceal mid hearpan æt his hlafordes fotum sittan, feoh ðicgan and a suellice snere wræstan, lætan scralletan scearo se ðe hleapeð nægl *neomegende*.

Nihtsang: 1. the book containing the service for compline. 2. compline, see *PMLA*.
> *CD.* 4. 275: And nu ða synd .ii. fulle mæssebec and .i. collectaneum and .ii. fulle sangbec and .i. *nihtsang*.

Nōnsang: none, see *PMLA*.

Ofersingan: to sing over a person.
> *C. Æ.* 32: Gyf hwa bið geuntrumod betwux eow, he hate gefeccan him to ðære gelaðunge mæssepreostas, and by him *ofersingon* and him fore gebiddon.

Offerenda: the offertory anthem (L. offertorium).
> *Herr. Arch.* 29: Man æfter ðam godspelle ðone *offerendan* singe and æfter ðære offrunge ðam sacerde ða selfan palmtwiga offrige.

Offringsang: the offertory anthem.
> *Æ. H.* 1, 218. 9: Nu sceole we healdan urne palm, oð ðæt se sangere onginne ðone *offringsang*, and geoffrian ðonne Gode ðone palm.

Ontemn, see Antifen.

Organ: a song, canticle: a song with vocal accompaniment.
> *Sal.* 65: gif he æfre ðæs *organes* owiht cuðe, 107, (figuratively used of the Pater Noster); *Eccl. Inst.* (pref.) *organa* sweg ðe from englum bið sungen.

Organa? organe?: a musical instrument. a pipe organ?
> *Zu. Ap.* 32. 17: Da *organa* wæron getogene, and ða biman geblawene; *Ph.* 136: Ne magon ðam brealtme byman ne hornas, ne hearpan hlyn ne *organon*, ne ænig ðara dreama, ðe dryhten gescop gumum to gliwe in ðas geomran woruld; *Genesis* 4. 21: Jubal wæs fæder herpera and ðæra ðe *organan* macodun (L. pater canentium cithara et organo).

In translation from the Scriptures.
> Organum: *V. Ps.* 136. 2; 150. 4; *C. Ps.* 150. 4; *Th. Ps.* 136. 2.

Organistre: an organist.
> *Genesis* (Chase) 4. 21: And iubal wæs sangera fæder and hearpera and *organystra*: pater canentium cithara et organo.

Orgeldrēam: music of the organ.
> *Blick. Gl.*: *orgeldreame*: organo.

Orgenadrēam: music of the organ (L. organum).
Spl. Ps. 150. 4: Heriað hine on strengum and orgenadream.

Orgnian: to accompany a song.
Æ. Gr. 181. 2: ic undersinge oððe orgnige: succino.

Pīpdrēam: music of the pipe, piping.
Lchdm. 3. 208. 22: Pipdram singan gehyreð gehende blisse.

Pīpe: 1. a pipe. 2. a bagpipe.
Æ. Gl. 302. 5: pipe oððe hwistle: musa.
(?) CD. 4. 275: Đonne ys ðis sco onenawennis ðe he hæfð God mid gecnawen and sanctum Petrum into ðam halgan mynstre on cirelicum madwum, ðæt is ðæt he hætð ðiderynn gedon .v. silfrene caliceas and .iiii. corporales and .i. silfren pipe; W. H. 46. 16: Hearpe and pipe and mistlice gliggamen dremað eow on beorsele.

Pīpere: a piper.
Æ. Gr. 40. 8: pipere oððe hwistlere: tibicen; Æ. Gl. 302. 5: pipere: tibicen; W. W. 279. 5: pipere: tibicen.
Rush. Mt. 9. 23: Se Hælend geseah piperas (L. tibicines).

Pīplīc: musical.
Hpt. Gl. 445. 21: piplic: musica.

Plegean: to play on an instrument, [to sport].
V. Ps. 67. 26: in midle iungra plægiendra timpanan (L. tympanistriarum); C. Ps. 67. 26.

Prīmsang: prime, see PMLA.

Psealm, see Sealm.

Psaltere, see Saltere.

Psaltērium: a psaltery.
In translation from the Scriptures.
Psalterium: C. Ps. 32. 2; Th. Ps. 56. 10; 91. 3; 107. 2; 143. 10; 149. 3.

Rēodpipere: a player on a reed pipe.
W. W. 190. 7: reodpipere: auledus.

Reps: a response, psalm or portion of a psalm sung or read antiphonally in connection with the lessons in the services (L. responsorium).
Gr. BR. 39. 8: ðæt sealmas and antefnas and ræpsas and rædinga syn gesungenne, ðe to ðam freolsdæge belimpað, 20: Ræpsas ne syn næfre gesungene mid alleluian, butan fram eastran oð pentecosten; 41. 11: Æfter ðam sealmum sy anes capitules ræding geeweden, and siððan reps; BR. 45. 18; DCM. 552, 889: ðonne seo ðridde byð geræd ræding, . . . and ðænne se ðridda byð gesungen reps; 941; Herr. Arch. 26: ðam sangere ðisne reps beginnende, 'Ingrediente domino'; see DCM., BR., Gr. BR., for further refs.

Ringan, see Hringan.

Sǣlēoð: a sea-song, song of the rowers in keeping time.
W. W. 379. 9: *sæleoðcs*: celeumatis.

Sælterium: a psaltery (L. psalterium).
C. Ps. 91. 3: *sælterio*.

Salletan: to accompany sacred song with the harp (L. psallere).
Th. Ps. 194. 2: Singað him and *salletað*.

Saltere: 1. the Psalter, a book containing the psalms arranged for service (L. psalterium). 2. a selection of psalms from the psalter (L. psalterium). 3. a psaltery, stringed musical instrument (L. psalterium). 4. [the Book of Psalms.]
H. W. 278. 11: *saltere*: sambucus.

I. The Psalter.
BR. 51. 14; *Gr. BR.* 44. 16: ða hundteontigandfiftig ðæs *salteres* sealmas, 20; *DCM.* 362; *Byrht.* 333. 43; *Æ. PE.* 44: Mæssepreost sceal habban *saltere*; *C. Æ.* 21; *CD.* 4. 275; *Lchdm.* 3. 166. 22; 288. 13; *Techmer* 2. 121. 7.

II. A selection of psalms.
DCM. 679: Dysum ðrim dagum prime gedonum hi sungan *sealtere*; *Shrn.* 134. 17: He asong ælce dæge tuwa his *saltere* and his mæssan; *W. H.* 181. 21; *Herr. Arch.* 111. 112.

III. A psaltery.
Lchdm. 3. 302. 14: cimbalan oððe *psalteras* oððe strengas ætrinan saca hit getacnað.

In translation from the Scriptures.
Psalterium: *C. Ps.* 56. 9; 80. 3; 107. 3; 143. 9, 11; 149. 3; 150. 3; *Spl. Ps.* 32. 2; 56. 11; 80. 2; 91. 3; 107. 2; 149. 3; 150. 3; *Th. Ps.* 107. 2.

IV. [The Book of Psalms.]
ONT. 7. 26 (Ælfric's explanation): Se *saltere* ys an boc ðe he gesette ðurh God betwux oðrum bocum on ðære bibliothecan.

Sang: 1. song, singing, (generic). 2. a song, hymn, psalm, lay to be sung or recited, (specific). [noise, poem, lay.]
W. W. 129. 20: sarlic *sang*: trenos, 28: twegra *sang*: bicinium, 31: bluddra *sang*: chorea, 38: ungeswege *sang*: diaphonia, 39: sum *swegesang*: canticum, 43: geðwære *sang*: armonia, 44: answege *sang*: simphonia; *Hpt. Gl.* 415. 22: mid swið swinum *sangum* dreames, 1 heringe: dulcisonis melodiae; 416. 22: *sangum*: concentibus (gl. cantibus, melodiis); 467. 4: twinnum *sangum*: geminis concentibus (gl. cantibus), 5: *sang*: melodia (gl. cantilena, laude); 519. 6; *sangum*: carminibus; 17: gedremere swinsunge (marg. gedremum *sange*): consona melodia; *Napier Gl.* 64: *sang*: armonia.

I. Song, singing, [noise], (generic sense).
A. Sacred song.
1. Of mortals.
Æ. LS. 21. 227: Hi ealle eodon endemes to cyrcan and mid *sange*

heredon ðæs sanctes mærða; 21.242; 22.71; *Æ. H.* 2.312.7; 518.28: Mid gastlicum *sange* ðone sanct ferodon to ðære ylcan byrig ðe he on biscop wæs, 30; *Gr. Pr.* 3.9.384: And hi hereodon ða god mid swiðlicre blisse on *sange* and on dreame; *El.* 867: Gesæton sigcrofe, *sang* ahofon rædðeahtende ymb ða roda ðreo oð ða nigoðan tid; *Æ. Gr.* 279.5: Dæt leoð getacnode godes ðeowena *sang*.

2. Of heavenly beings.

Æ. LS. 20.130: Drihtnes englas feredon his sawle mid *sange* to heofonum; 29.301; *Æ. H.* 1.38.7: Hi calle samod mid gedremum *sange* Godes wuldor hleoðrodon; 442.1, 2; 2.150.27; 518.10: twa heofenlice werod ætforan ðære cytan dura, singende heofenlicne *sang*; *ONT.* 13.17; *Bd.* 266.26; *An.* 869: Ðær wæs singal *sang* and swegles gong, wlitig weoroda heap and wuldres ðreat; *Chr.* 502, 1050: Dær is engla *song*, eadigra blis; *Sat.* 45, 143: Is me nu wyrsæ, ðæt ic wuldres leoht uppe mid englum æfre cuðe, *song* on swegle, ðær sunu meotodes habbað cadigne bearn calle ymbfangen, seolfa mid *sange*; 235, 663; *Shrn.* 29.27: Da hirdas gehirdon micelne engla *sang*; 59.13.

B. Secular song.

1. Glees and joyful music.

Zu. Ap. 27.13: Heo mid winsumum *sange* gemægnde ðare hearpan sweg, 29; 28.28; *B.* 90, 1063: Dær wæs *sang* and sweg samod ætgædere fore Healfdenes hildewisan, gomenwudu greted, gid oft wrecen, ðonne healgamen Hroðgares scop æfter medobence mænan scolde; *Scop.* 67: Me ðær Guðhere forgeaf glædlicne maððum *songes* to leane, 100—108: Me ða Ealhhild oðerne forgeaf, dryhtewen dugude, dohtor Eadwines. Hyre lof lengde geond londa fela, ðonne ic be *songe* secgan sceolde, hwær ic under swegle selast wisse goldhrodene cwen giefe bryttian. Donne wit Scilling sciran reorde for uncrum sigedryhtne *song* ahofan, hlude bi hearpan hleoðor swinsade: ðonne monige men modum wlonce wordum sprecan, ða ðe wel cuðan, ðæt hi næfre *song* sellan ne hyrdon.

2. Songs of sorrow and mourning.

B. 787: sigeleasne *sang*, sar wanigean hellehæfton; 2417: Donne he gyd wrece, sarigne *sang*, ðonne his sunu hangað hrefne to hroðre and he him helpan ne mæg.

C. Song ascribed to birds and animals.

Seaf. 19: Hwilum ylfete *song*; *R.* 58.3: *Sanges* rofe heapum ferað, hlude cirmað; 25.6; *El.* 29: Earn *sang* ahof laðum on laste; 112: wulf *sang* ahof; *Ph.* 337: Donne fugla cynn on healfa gehwone heapum ðringað, signd sidwegum, *songe* lofiað, mærað modigne meaglum reordum; *Met.* 13.50. *St. Gu.* 528.10.

D. Music of an instrument.

G. PC. 175.9: Ealle [hearpan strengas] he [se hearpere] gret mid anre honda, ðy ðe he wile ðæt hi anne *song* singen, ðeah he hie ungelice styrige.

II. **A song, hymn, psalm, lay to be sung or recited, (specific).**
   A. **A sacred song.**
      1. **Of mortals.**
         a) Hymn.
   Æ. LS. 3. 632: Da com mycel meniu on mergen to ðam lice, and gebrohten ðæt lic, mid gastlicum *sangum*, into godes cyrccan; 20. 99; 21. 244, 264; *Bd.* 284. 15.
         b) Mass.
   W. H. 228. 29: gað to minum cyricum mid ælmessum and mid leohte and gehcrað ðone halgan *sang* and forlætað eorre and druncennesse; *BH.* 45. 36: Se biscop and se mæssepreost sceolan mæssan gesingan ... and ða ðe on heofenum syndon, hi ðingiað for ða ðe ðyssum *sange* fylgeað.
         c) Psalm.
   Æ. LS. 11. 106: sungan sona ðisne *sang* mid geleafan: Qui tribulant me inimici mei ipsi infirmati sunt et ceciderunt.
         d) The course of church music.
   Bd. 150. 31: He wæs monigra magister ciriclices sanges æfter Romane ðeawe and Cantwara; 258. 26; 314. 18: in his mynstre ðone *song* læran to twelf monðum ðe he æt Sce Petre geleornade, 20: endebyrdnesse and ðeaw ðæs *songes* cwicre stefne sangeras lærde; *Chad* 37.
         e) Litany, Pater Noster, and Creed.
   Lchdm. 2. 138. 18, 20; 356. 8.
         f) Unclassified.
   Æ. LS. 3. 136; 11. 164; *Herr. Arch.* 42.
      2. **Of heavenly beings.**
   Æ. LS. 15. 212: And hi sungon ðisne *sang* mid singalum dreame, 'Sanctus, sanctus, sanctus dominus deus omnipotens; *Æ. H.* 2. 86. 34; 342. 11; *Gr. Pr.* 3. 2. 117, 129; 3. 465—468: Da oðre halgan magon gehyran ðone *sang*, ðe ða mædenu singað mid swiðlicum dreame, and hi habbað ða blisse ðæs heofonlican *sanges*, ðeah ðe hi singan ne magon ðone *sang* swa swa hi; 2. 469, 471, 479; *G. PC.* 409. 8, 10, 12; *Bd.* 264. 21; 266. 23, 29; *Chad* 138, 142, 143; *Gu.* 1297.

   B. **A secular song.**
      1. **Glees and joyful music.**
   W. H. 148. 3: and ða caran aslawjað, ða ðe ær wæron ful swifte and hræde to gehyrenne fægere dreamas and *sangas*.
      2. **Marriage song.**
   Æ. LS. 34. 23.
      3. **Songs of sorrow and mourning.**
   C. Æ. 35: Ðonne forbeode ge ða hæðenan *sangas* ðæra læwedra manna: and heora hludan cheahchetunga.

C. [A lay or poem.]
Bt. 76.6; Apstls. 1; G. PC. 335. 23: ðæs psalmscopes *sang* ðe he sang.

III. Doubtful references. (It is uncertain whether the following should be classed under 'I A' or 'II A'.)
Æ. LS. 21. 234; Æ. H. 2. 98. 3, 6; 334. 12, 16; 342. 8; 548. 14(2), 16.

IV. In translation from the Scriptures and hymns.
Canticum: V. Ps. 32. 3; 39. 4; 68. 31; 91. 4; 95. 1; 97. 1; 136. 3, 4; 137. 5; 143. 9; 149. 1; C. Ps. 32. 3; 39. 4; 68. 31; 95. 1; 97. 1; 137. 5; 143. 9; 149. 1; Spl. Ps. 91. 3; 143. 11; Th. Ps. 32. 3; 39. 2; 95. 1; 136. 4(2); 137. 5; 149. 1. Cantio: V. Ps. 136. 3; Spl. Ps. 136. 3. Cantatio: Spl. Ps. 70. 8. Decantatio: V. Ps. 70. 6; C. Ps. 70. 6. Cantus: A. S. H. 57. 9; 132. 3. Jubilatio: Th. Ps. 46. 5. Concentus: A. S. H. 73. 7. Chorus: Lind. Lk. 15. 25. Cantabiles mihi erant justificationes: Th. Ps. 118. 54: Ac me to *sange* symble hæfde, hu ic ðine soðfæstnesse selest heolde; C. Ps. 118. 54. (There is no Latin equivalent for the following): Th. Ps. 41. 9; 42. 5; 149. 1.

Sangbōc: 1. a singing-book with the notes marked. 2. the church singing-book containing the hymns and canticles.

I. A singing-book with notes.
Æ. Gr. 291. 11: Ðæra mearcunga sind manega and mislice gesceapne, ægðer ge on *sangbocum* ge on leoðcræfte.

II. The church singing-book.
Æ. PE. 44: Mæssepreost sceal habban mæsseboc, *sangbec* and rædingebec; C. Æ. 21; CD. 4. 275: Ðær næron ær buton .ii. fulle mæssebec and .i. collectaneum and .ii. pistelbec and .ii. fulle *sangbec*.

Sangcræft: 1. the art of singing. 2. any form of music. [the art of writing poetry].
Hpt. Gl. 479. 9: *sangcræft*: musica.

I. The art of singing.
Bd. 260. 19: Wæs he swiðost in cirican *songcræft* getyd Romanisce ðeawe, ðone he geleornade from Sēē Gregories discipulum.

II. Any form of music.
Ph. 132: Bið ðæs hleoðres sweg eallum *songcræftum* swetra and wlitigra and wynsumra wrenca gehwylcum. Ne magon ðam breahtme byman ne hornas, ne hearpan hlyn ne hæleða stefn ænges on eorðan ne organan, swegleoðres geswin ne swanes feðre, ne ænig ðara dreama, ðe dryhten gescop gumum to gliwe in ðas geomran woruld.

III. [The art of writing poetry.]
Bd. 342. 15: He ðurh Godes gife ðone *sangcræft* onfeng.

Sangdrēam: music, a portion of song (L. cantilena).
DCM. 638: hwæt to *sangdreame* ðære nihte gebyrige.

Sangere: 1. a singer (generic sense). 2. a leader of the church music.
W. W. 150. 16: idel *sangere*: temelici; Æ. Gr. 71. 6: *sangere*: cantor; 216. 4: *sangere*: cantor; Æ. Gl. 299. 14: *sangere*: cantor.

I. A singer.
Genesis (Chase) 4. 20: Jubal was *sangera* fæder.

II. A leader of the music.
BH. 207. 31: Se bisceop ðær gesette gode *sangeras* and mæssepreostas and manigfealdlice circiccan ðeguas; (c) Bd. 258. 26: ond ærest buton Jacobe ðæm *songere* wæs songes magister Ædde haten; 314. 21; Æ. H. 1. 218. 9: oððæt se *sangere* onginne ðone offringsang; 508. 27; L. Eth. 7; DCM. 627; BR. 38. 13; Gr. BR 33. 16; Herr. Arch. 26.

Sangestre: a songstress.
Æ. Gr. 71. 6: *sangestre*: cantrix.

Sangpīpe: a bagpipe?
Prud. Gl. 389. 26: *sangpipe*: camena.

Sārga: a trumpet.
Æ. Gl. 302. 8: trnðhorn oðð e *sarga*: lituus; Hpt. Gl. 445. 21: *sargana*: salpicum (gl. tubarum) tubicanatorum.

Sceacel: a plectrum.
W. W. 466. 28: *sceecle*: plectro; 517. 2: *sceacelas*: plectra.

Scearu: a plectrum (?).
Fates of Men. 83: Sum sceal mid hearpan æt his hlafordes fotum sittan, feoh ðicgan and a snellice snere wræstan, lætan scralletan *scearo* se ðe hleapeð nægl neomegende.

Scēawendwīse: a buffoon's song (?).
R. 9. 9: Saga, hwæt ic hatte, ðe swa scirenige *sceawendwisan* hlude onhyrge, hæleðum bodige wilcumena fela woðe minre.

Scecel, see Sceacel.

Scop: a singer, [ballad reciter].
B. 90: Dær wæs hearpan sweg, swutol sang *scopes*, 496: Scop hwilum sang hador on Heorote, 1066; Deor 36.

Scralletan: to sound shrilly.
Fates of Men 83: Sum sceal mid hearpan æt his hlafordes fotum sittan, feoh ðicgan and a snellice snere wræstan, lætan *scralletan* scearo se ðe hleapeð nægl neomegende.

Scyll: resonant, [acute].
Rim. P. 27: *Scyl* wæs hearpe.

Scypbȳme: a trumpet used on ship.
Prud. Gl. 391. 48: *scypbyman*: classicam tubam.

Sealm: 1. a psalm from the Psalter. 2. a sacred song. (L. psalmus).
Blick. Gl.: sealm: psalmum.
I. A psalm.
BR. 42.10: syx and syxteogaða *sealm* buton antempne, 12; *Gr. BR.* 33.13: syx *sealmas* mid ðrim antefnum, 22: Æfterfyligan oðre syx *sealmas* and ða syn gesungene mid 'Alleluia'; *CD.* 5.113; *St. Gu.* 18.7,13; *DCM.* 269: Oððe seofon dædbote *sealmas*, 561: Geendedum ðrim rædinegum syx nocternes ðæs æftran *sealmas* swa ða ærran mid ðrim antefnum of ðære sealma sange gesettnm beon gesungene; *Herr. Arch.* 77: Forðrihte sy gesungen canonica tidsangas todæledum *sealmum* æfter heora ðeawe. See *Singan* I. A.13 for further references.

II. A song.
ONT. 7.25: David witegode fela ymbe Crist, swa swa us cyðað ða *sealmas* ðe he gesang.

In translation from the Scriptures.
'Psalmum dicere' translated by '*sealm* singan': *Th. Ps.* 56.9,11; 67.4; 107.3; 146.1. 'Psallere' translated by '*sealm* singan': *Spl. Ps.* 107.3.

Sealmbōc: the book of psalms.
Æ. H. 1.604.24: swa swa se ylca apostol ðisum wordum tæhte, 'Donne ge eow to gereorde gaðeriað, habbe eower gehwilc halwende lare on muðe, and *sealmboc* on handa'.

Sealmcwide: psalmody (L. psalmus).
Lamb. Ps. 97.5: on stefne *sealmewides*.

[Sealmfæt]: mechanical translation of 'vasum psalmi'.
Th. Ps. 70.20: on *sealmfatum*.

Sealmgetæl: a tale or number of psalms.
Gr. BR. 43.19: Forðam ðe ðæs *sealmgetæles* is elles to lyt, ða ðry mæstan sealmas sculon beon todælede on twegen glorian.

Sealmglīg: psalmody.
Blick. Gl.: sealmglige: psalterio.
Lamb. Ps. 143.9: *sealmglywe*: psalterio.

Sealmian: to sing sacred music with a stringed accompaniment (psallere).
Spl. Ps. (M.) 107.1: Ic singe and *sealmige*.

Sealmlēoð: a psalm.
Bl. Gl.: sealmleoð and hearpsweg (L. psalterium et cythara).

Sealmlof: a psalm, psalmody.
Lamb. Ps. 17.50: *sealmlof*: psalmus; 97.4: *sealmlof* cweðað: psallite; 107.3: *sealmlof*: psalterium, 146.1: *sealmlof*: psalmus.

Sealmlofian: to sing sacred music with a stringed accompaniment (L. psallere).
Lamb. Ps. 104. 2: Singað him and sealmlofiað.

Sealmsang: 1. singing of psalms (L. psalmodia). 2. the Psalter (L. psalterium). 3. a psalm (L. psalmus). 4. [Book of Psalms.]

I. Singing of psalms.
W. W. 445. 40: sealmsang: melodiam; 224. 32: ðæs dæglican sealmsanges: diurne psalmodie.
BR. 39. 11: Æle swa swa hit her bufan gesett sealmsangas mycelnyss si gehealden; 47. 3; 51. 5; Gr. BR. 32. 17; 34. 9; 40. 19: Nu geo we habbað gefadod ða endebyrdnesse ðæs sealmsanges, ðe to uhtsange oððe dægredsange gebyreð; 44. 9; 44. 14; 45. 11: swa standan æt ðam scalmsange (L. ad psallendum), ðæt ure mod geðwærige mid ðæs mudes clypunge; BH. 199. 34; Æ. LS. 23 B. 36; Æ. H. 1. 188. 18: Da twegen fixas getacnodon sealmsang and ðæra witegena cwydas. An ðæra geeydde and bodode Cristes tocyme mid sealmsange, and oðer mid witegunge; Bd. 242. 33; 284. 9; W. H. 171. 13; 173. 22; 277. 6; DCM. 116, 130, 264, 376, 472, 543, 617, 1121; Byrht. 319. 43; Lchdm. 3. 166. 20; Judy. 5 (Ælfric's explanation); Shrn. 14. 7: Dær his drohtnunge and his sealmsanges on ðam wætere hnacodon leomen adreah swa his gewune wæs; Herr. Arch. 9.

II. The Psalter.
BR. 37. 9: Da scalmsanges oððe rædinge sum ðine beheofiað; 52. 5: ða læs sealmsanges mid lofsange mid gewunelicum iond ðære uwnean emrene singað.

III. A psalm.
a) Sung in services.
BR. 45. 12; 50. 18; Æ. LS. 23 B. 120: Hi ðonne ðisne sealmsang sungon togædere: Dominus illuminatio mea et salus mea quem timebo, 746; Æ. H. 1. 606. 20; on sealmsangum and gastlicum lofsangum, singende mid gife Godes on eowrum heortum; Bd. 340. 24; 350. 21.
B. In translation from the Scriptures and hymns.
Lamb. Ps. 146. 1; 60. 9; ASH. 7. 34.

IV. [The Book of Psalms.]
Æ. H. 1. 188. 16-19: Da twegen fixas getacnodon sealmsang and ðæra witegena cwydas.

[Sealmscop]: the psalmist.
BH. 105. 10; W. H. 250. 18; G. PC. 335. 22; Æ. H. 1. 118. 1; 410. 15: swa swa se sealmsceop be ðam gyddigende sang; 2. 82. 30.

[Sealmwyrhta]: the psalmist.
Æ. H. 2. 14. 32: Eft, be Cristes acennednysse Dauid se sealmwyrhta sang.

Sealtere, see Saltere.

Sigelēoð: a song of triumph.
I. A war song.
El. 124: Ða wæs ðuf hafen, segn for sweotum, *sigeleoð* galen;
II. A song of angels.
Gu. 1289: Ða wæs Guðlaces gæst gelæded eadig on upweg. Engla ðreatas *sigeleoð* sungon.

Singan: to sing (L. agere (a), canere (c), cantare (ct), celebrare (cl), decantare (dct), dicere (d), incantare, jubilare (j), modulari (m), occinere, peragere (pa), psallere (p), recitare (r), resonare), [recite, compose.]
Æ. Gr. 177. 16: ic *singe*: psallo; 180. 5: ic *singe*: cano; 192. 18: ic *singe* mine sealmas: psallo; 181. 3: ic *singe* ongean: occino; *Hpt. Gl.* 438. 20: he *sin(g)ð*: decantet.

I. Singing of sacred music.
A. By mortals.
1. Anthems.
(d) *BR.* 38. 6, 8; (d) 43. 8; (d) 45. 7; *Gr. BR.* 39. 8: Sealmas and antefenas syn *gesungene*; (c) *DCM.* 240, (dct) 243, (c) 500, (c) 549, (dct) 550, (c) 568, (c) 571, (c) 631, (c) 690, (c) 809, (ct) 858, (c) 860, (c) 898, (c) 922, (c) 975; (c) *Herr. Arch.* 29: Man æfter ðam godspelle ðone offerendan *singe*, 44, (c) 127.

2. Services of the canonical hours.
(c) *DCM.* 370, (c) 385, (ct) 410, (p) 476, (c) 510, (ct) 694, (cl) 711, (c) 823, (cl) 864, (dct) 950, (c) 955, (ps) 1017; (?) *Æ. H.* 1. 508. 33; *Æ. LS.* 19. 24; *Æ. PF.* 31; *C. Æ.* 19, 36 (4); (a) *Herr. Arch.* 37, (d) 79, 81, (d) 87, 106, (ct) 133, 198, (a) 200; *Bd.* 348. 14: ða broður arisan scolden and Godes lof ræran and heora uhtsong *singan*.

3. Canticles.
(p) *BR.* 41. 6; (p) 44. 3, (d) 3; (d) 45. 17; 52. 3; *Gr. BR.* 39. 19; 44. 19; *BH.* 5. 8; 7. 1; 159. 1; *Æ. H.* 1. 202. 24—25: Ða *sang* Maria ðærrihte ðone lofsang ðe we *singað* on Godes cyrcan, æt ælcum æfensange, 'Magnificat anima mea Dominum'; *Lchdm.* 2. 346. 11, 18; 3. 14. 25; 62. 21.

4. Chants.
(ct) *Bd.* 258. 24: Swylce eac sonas to *singenne* in circan, ða ðe oððæt in Cent anre menn cuðon, of ðære tide ongunnon men leornian ðurh calle ciricau Ongolcynnes.

5. Creed.
W. H. 35. 8; *Æ. LS.* 5. 359; 17. 96; *Eccl. Inst.* 478, 481 (2); *Lchdm.* 2. 186. 4; 346. 5, 24; 356. 6.

6. Doxologies.
  a. Alleluia.
    (c) *BR.* 39. 4; 45. 11; (c) *DCM.* 860, (ct) 1011, (c) 1019; *BH.* 149. 23; *Æ. H.* 2. 88. 6: We him *singað* ecelice Alleluian butan geswince; 122. 5.
  b. Gloria in excelsis Deo.
    (c) *DCM.* 538, (ct) 850, (c) 1019; (det) *Herr. Arch.* 22; *Lchdm.* 2. 116. 16: *Sing* .xii. siðum ðone scalm 'Miserere mei deus', and 'Gloria in excelsis deo'; 346. 24.
  c. Gloria laus.
    (det) *DCM.* 626: Cildru ða beforan codan *singan* (gloria laus).
  d. Gloria patri.
    (d) *BR.* 38. 13; (d) 40. 14; *Gr. BR.* 33. 16; 35. 10; ðonne me 'Gloria patri' *singe.*

7. Hymns.
  (d) *BR.* 41. 11; *Gr. BR.* 33. 12; 40. 23; (d) *DCM.* 446, (p) 446, (d) 448, (cl) 452, (det) 454, (cl) 456, (ct) 503, (cl) 509 (2), (c) 529, (c) 756, (c) 860, (c) 1023; *BH.* 147. 3; 151. 29; *W. H.* 237. 20; *Æ. H.* 1. 150. 29, 30; 214. 4, 9, 16; 218, 4; 2. 294. 1: Ðillice ne magon *singan* ðone lofsang 'Ðes is se dæg ðe Drihten worhte'; *Æ. LS.* 21. 230, 233, 236, 246, 259, 264; 28. 82; *Herr. Arch.* 149; *Gr. Pr.* 3. 2. 28; *Shrn.* 49. 18.

8. Lessons.
  (r) *BR.* 39. 6, (d) 6; (d) 45. 7; *Gr. BR.* 39. 8.

9. Litanies and prayers.
  Gr. BR. 38. 17; (c) *DCM.* 848, (c) 1007: Niðerga se abbud mid scole *singendre* (letanias) fitfealde to fantum bletsigenne; *W. H.* 20. 18; 171. 15; 290. 13; *Æ. H.* 2. 126. 12, 20; 136. 16; 138. 5, 8: Ða dyde Cuðberhtus swa his gewuna wæs, *sang* his gebedn on sælicere yðe, standende oð ðone swyran; *Æ. LS.* 13. 83; 29. 231; (m) *Bd.* 58. 26; (m) 60. 18; (a) *Herr. Arch.* 13, (p) 46, (a) 113, 206; *Lchdm.* 2. 112. 27; 138. 7: Se mæssepreost him *singe* æfter ðam drence ðis ofer: 'Domine sancte pater omnipotens', 17; 346. 5, 11, 18, 24; 356. 6.

10. Mass.
  (cl) *DCM.* 325, (cl) 350, (cl) 489, (cl) 523, (c) 613, (cl) 687, (cl) 951, (cl) 952, (cl) 1134; *Æ. H.* 1. 74. 22: On ðam sunnanuhtan ærwacol to ðære cyrcan com, and ðam folce mæssan *gesang*; 508. 3; 2. 358. 15; *Æ. LS.* 4. 230; *Æ. Coll.* 101. 31; *C. Æ.* 36, (c) *Herr. Arch.* 3, 121, (cl) 146; *Klgk.* 7. 12; *Eccl. Inst.* 471, 472, 473, 488 (2); *CD.* 1. 293 (2); 4. 282; *SC.* 156. 3; 250. 15; 255. 23; *Lchdm.* 1. 398. 16; 2. 138. 2, 10, 20, 28; 140. 13; 142. 8; 334. 14; 346. 1; 356, 9; 3. 6. 31; 12. 5; 28. 16; 46. 17; *Shrn.* 74. 27; 98. 21.

11. Pater Nosters.
W. H. 20. 16; 36. 24; 143. 11; *Æ. LS.* 5. 359; 17. 96; *Eccl. Inst.*
478, 481; *Sal.* 171, 333; *Lchdm.* 1. 393. 18; 394. 2; 2. 112, 27; 116.
13, 16; 136. 4; 138. 17; 346. 5, 11, 18, 24; 356. 6; 358. 11, 12; 3. S. 30;
38. 10; 68. 31; 74. 14, 16; *Lorica Prayer* 9.

12. Praise, songs of praise.
Æ. H. 1. 56. 27; 2. 200. 20: We ðonne sigefæste, mid geleafan
Godes lof singað; *Æ. LS.* 11. 164, 231; 32. 23; *Harr. H.* 102.

a. The singing of the Psalmist.
BH. 105. 10; *W. H.* 250. 18; *G. PC.* 335. 22; *Æ. H.* 1. 118. 1;
410. 15: swa swa se scalmsceop be ðam gyddigende *sang.*

13. Psalms.
(d) *BR.* 38. 1, (d) 6, (d) 8; (c) 39. 4; (d) 40. 3; (d) 42. 10, (d)
12; (d) 43. 4, (d) 7, (d) 8; (d) 45. 7, (d) 14; (d) 48. 7, (d) 18; (d)
49. 1, (d) 11, (p) 15; (p) 50. 6, (d) 12; (p) 51. 16; (p) 52. 4; (d) 77, 2;
Gr. BR. 33. 22; 34. 15; 35. 6, 10; 36. 12; 39. 8; 41. 9; 42. 4, 7, 11;
42. 23; 43. 18; 44. 1, 13, 18, 20; *Judg.* 5 [Ælfric's explanation], 8 [Æ.
cx.]; *ONT.* 7. 25; (p) *DCM.* 186, (det) 194, (d) 201, (d) 208, (c) 216,
(c) 249, (c) 256, (p) 270, (det) 313, (c) 355, (c) 370, (c) 415, (det)
563, (det) 771, (det) 816, (c) 906, (c) 922, (det) 924, (c) 976, (c) 1106,
(c) 1129; *W. H.* 181. 27; 171. 14; *Æ. H.* 2. 16. 32; 98. 1: ðæt hi
astodon, and on his forðsiðe heora sealmas *sungon*, 2; *Æ. LS.* 5.
391; 11. 43, 85, 106, 116, 119, 249; 23. 436; 23 B. 120; *Eccl. Inst.* 481;
(c) *Bd.* 66. 5; (c) 416. 13; (c) 444. 10; *St. Gu.* 26. 21; 28. 20; 44. 1;
44. 3; *Byrht.* 332. 37; *Lchdm.* 2. 116. 16; 136. 4; 138. 4; 292. 2; 352.
14; 3. 12. 6; 14. 25; 24. 21; 56. 9; 166. 24; (d) *Herr. Arch.* 76, (d)
78, (d) 98, (d) 99, (p) 111.

14. Responses.
(d) *BR.* 45. 18; *Gr. BR.* 39. 8; (c) *DCM.* 552, (cl) 880, (c) 941.

15. Verses.
(d) *BR.* 77. 8; *Gr. BR.* 35. 7: *Singe* man ærest six sealmas and
ðonne on ende *fers*, 11; (det) *DCM.* 704.

16. References to the absolute use.
BR. 38. 12: se ðe *singe*; 81. 2; *Gr. BR.* 45. 8, 9; *BH.* 77. 15;
81. 27; 149. 30; 157. 31; 231, 9; 237. 23; *W. H.* 152. 13, 25; 153. 2;
Æ. H. 1. 546. 15; 2. 292. 33; *Æ. LS.* 1. 191, 192 (2), 194; 23 B. 164,
165; *G. PC.* 347. 6.

B. By heavenly beings.
1. Praises to God.
ONT. 19. 13; *Gr. Pr.* 3. 2. 117, 118; 3. 460, 161, 466, 468, 469, 479;
Æ. LS. 15. 212: Hi *sungon* ðisne sang mid singalum dreame, Sanctus,
Sanctus, Sanctus, dominus deus omnipotens; *Æ. H.* 1. 38. 10; 90. 3;
Chr. 388: Seraphimes cynn uppe mid englum a bremende unaðreo-

tendum ðrymmum *singað* ful healice hludan stefne; *Sat.* 355; *Lord's Pr.* 54; *Ph.* 617, 635; *El.* 746; *An.* 877.

2. Songs at the death of a saint.

Chr. 685; *Gu.* 1289; *Æ. H.* 2. 334. 12; 548. 10: Efne ða, æfter ðære huslunge, stodon twa heofenlice werod ætforan ðære cytan dura, *singende* heofenliene sang, and hi tocneowon ðæt werhades men ongunnon symle ðone dream, and wifhades men him *sungon* ongean, andswariende; *Æ. LS.* 29. 297, 300.

3. Songs for Christ the bridegroom.

Æ. LS. 7. 44: His brydbedd me is gearo nu in mid dreamum, his mædenu me *singað* mid geswegum stemnum.

II. Singing of secular music.
A. Glees and popular song.

Gr. Pr. 3. 11. 129; 23. 540; *B.* 496: Scop hwilum *sang* hador on Heorote; *Scop.* 54: Forðon ic mæg *singan* and secgan spell, mænan fore mengo in meoduhealle, hu me cynegode cystum dohten; *Chr.* 667; *Shrn.* 121. 7; *Bd.* 342. 22.

B. Incantations and charms.

Lchdm. 1. 390. 17; 392. 7, 9, 10; 393. 18; 2. 136. 4; 304. 2, 4, 9, 10; 322. 6; 348. 26; 350. 28; 352. 4, 5; 3. 8. 18; 10. 11, 13, 16, 17, 18; 24. 25, 28; 38. 3, 5; 174. 10; 286. 1, 3, 5; 288. 13, 14, 17, 18, 20; 294. 6.

III. Singing of birds.

Ph. 124: swa se haswa fugel, swinsað and *singeð* swegle togeanes; 140; *Fin.* 6; *Gen.* 1983; *Seaf.* 22: Dyde ic me to gomene ganetes hleoðor and huilpan sweg fore hleahtor wera, mæw *singende* fore medodrince, 54; *Judith* 211; *Sal.* 539; *R. S. S*; 9. 2 (pipe or nightingale according to the interpretation of the riddle, vv. 6—8 favor pipe).

IV. Sounding of instruments (more or less figuratively used).

B. 1423: Horn stundum *song* fuslic fyrðleoð; *G. PC.* 175. 8, 9; *Lchdm.* 3. 208. 22; *Exod.* 132, 160, 565; *Dan.* 192; *El.* 109; *By.* 284; *R.* 9. 2, (pipe or nightingale according to the interpretation of the riddle; vv. 6—8 favor pipe); *Shrn.* 82. 22.

V. Unclassified references.

Æ. LS. 3. 340; *Exod.* 164: Wulfas *sungon* atol æfenleoð ætes on wenan.

VI. In translation from the Scriptures.

Psallere: *V. Ps.* 7. 18; 9. 3, 12; 12. 6; 20. 14; 29. 5; 32. 2, 3; 46. 7 (4), 8; 58. 18; 60. 9; 65. 4; 67. 26, 33 (2); 68. 13; 70. 22; 91. 2; 97. 4, 5; 100, 1; 103. 33; 104. 2; 134. 3; 137. 1; 143. 9; 145. 2; 146. 7; 149, 3; *C. Ps.* 7. 18; 9. 3, 12; 12. 6; 29. 5; 32. 2, 3; 46. 7 (4), 8; 58. 18; 60. 9; 65. 4; 67. 26, 33 (2); 68. 13; 70. 22; 91. 1; 97. 4, 5; 100. 1; 103. 33; 104. 2; 134. 3; 137. 1; 143. 9; 145. 2; 146. 7; 149. 3; *Spl. Ps.* 7. 18; 9. 2, 11; 12. 6; 29. 4; 32. 2, 3; 46. 6, 7; 58. 20; 65. 3; 67. 27,

Singan — Sōn]   Glossary.   99

35, 36; 68. 15; 70. 24; 91. 1; 97. 5, 6; 100. 1; 103. 34; 104. 2; 107. 3;
134. 3; 137. 2; 143. 11; 145. 1; 146. 7; 149. 3; *Th. Ps.* 46. 6, 7; 58.
17; 60. 6; 65. 4; 67. 24; 70. 20; 100. 1; 103. 31; 137. 1; 143. 10; 145,
1; 146. 1, 7; 149. 3; *Ps.* 46. 8 (*BR.* 52. 15); 137. 1 (*BR.* 52. 16); 59.
17 (*Æ. H.* 2. 82. 31).—Cantare: *V. Ps.* 20. 14; 26. 6; 32. 3; 56. 8;
58. 17; 67. 5, 33; 70. 8; 74. 10; 88. 2; 95. 1, 2; 97. 1, 4; 100. 1; 103.
33; 104. 2; 105. 12; 107. 2; 136. 3, 4; 137. 5; 143. 9; 149, 1; *C. Ps.*
20. 14; 26. 6; 32. 3; 56. 8; 58. 17; 67. 5, 33; 70. 8; 74, 10; 88, 2; 95.
1, 2; 97. 1, 4; 100. 1; 103. 33; 104. 2; 105. 12; 107. 2; 136. 3 (2), 4 (2);
137. 5; 143, 9; 149. 1; *Spl. Ps.* 20. 13; 26. 11; 32. 3; 56. 10; 58. 18;
67. 4, 35; 70. 9; 74. 9; 88. 1; 95. 1 (2), 2; 97. 1, 5; 100. 1; 103. 34;
104. 2; 107. 1; 136. 4, 5; 137. 6; 143. 11; 149. 1; *Th. Ps.* 12. 6; 26, 7;
32. 3; 58. 16; 67. 4; 70. 7; 74. 8; 88. 1; 95. 1 (2), 2; 100. 1; 103. 31;
104. 2; 136. 4, 5; 137. 5; 143. 10; 149. 1; *Ex.* 32. 18; *Skt. Lk.* 7. 32.—
Canere: *V. Ps.* 80. 4; *C. Ps.* 80. 4; *Ex.* 15. 1; *Lind. Mt.* 6. 2; *Lind.
Mt.* 11. 17; *Skt. Mt.* 11. 17.—Jubilare: *Spl. Ps.* 80. 1 (m).—Psalmum
dicere: *C. Ps.* 17. 50; *Spl. Ps.* 17. 51; *Th. Ps.* 17. 47; 56. 9, 11; 107.
3.—Incantare: *Th. Ps.* 57. 5.—Decantare: *Deut.* 31. 19.—Without
Latin equivalents: *C. Ps.* 91. 3; 94. 2; *Th. Ps.* 41. 9; 70. 5; 91. 3;
94. 2; 107. 2; 136. 4; 149. 1.

VII. In translation from the hymns.

Psallere: *ASH.* 4. 15; 18. 12; 26. 4; 56. 5; 57. 2; 60. 17; 61. 5;
146. 2.—Cantare: *ASH.* 45. 1; *Vesp. H.* 2. 8.—Canere: *ASH.* 2. 12;
5. 6; 7. 18; 8. 1; 9. 16; 14. 12; 18. 3; 22. 1; 33. 4; 51. 8; 55. 12; 56.
14; 59. 4; 60. 16; 72. 10; 73. 15; 82. 4; 87. 1; 115. 17; 121. 5; 122. 4;
123. 10, 11; 129. 11, 12; 134. 3; 137. 10; 139. 3; 140. 11; 144. 4; *Vesp.
H.* 12. 6.—Resonare: *ASH.* 72. 5.

Singendlīc: that may be sung (L. cantabilis).
V. Ps. 118. 54: *Singedlice* me werun rehtwisnisse ðine; *Spl. Ps.*
118. 54: ibid.

Slegel: a plectrum.
W. W. 466. 28: *slegele*: plectro.

Snēr: a harpstring.
Fates of Men 82: Sum sceal mid hearpan æt his hlafordes fotum
sittan, feoh ðicgan and a snellice *snere* wræstan; *Rim. P.* 25.

Sōn: 1. a chant, a tone.   2. music.   (L. sonus, canticum.)
I. An air, a song.

Bd. 258. 24: Swylce cac *sonas* to singenne in circan, ða ðe oððæt
in Cent anre menn cuðon, of ðære tide ongunnon men leornian ðurh
ealle cirican Ongolcynnes; *G. PC.* 175. 8: Ða hearpan strengas se
hearpere suiðe ungelice tichð and styreð and mid ðy geded ðæt hi
nawuht ungelice ðæm *sone* ne singað ðe he wilnað.

II. Music.

Gr. BR. 41. 9: Gif hit mycel gefcræden is, syn hy mid antefcne
gesungene, gif sco geferæden lytel is, syn hy forðrihte butan *sone*

7*

gesungene; *Bt.* 168. 23: Þa gehet he him ðæt, forðæm he wæs oflyst ðæs seldcuðan *sones.*

Sōncræft: music.
New Ald. Gl. 306: *soncræft*: musicam.

Song(-), see **Sang(-).**

? Sorhlēoð: a sorrowful lay.
B. 2460: Gewiteð ðonne on sealman, *sorhleoð* gæleð an æfter anum; *Rood.* 67: Ongunnon ða (after Christ's burial) *sorhleoð* galan.

Stefn: voice.
I. Literal use of the word.
Hpt. Gl. 467. 4: Mid dremere *stefne*; canora voce. *ASH.* 2. 14: De *stefn* gedryme (L. vox canora) swege; 7. 25; 115. 1: Mid gewilnungn *stefne* (L. votis voce) we singað, 15: Wuldor fæder gedrymum uton swegan mid *stefnum* (L. melodis vocibus); *DCM.* 675; *Herr. Arch.* 46, 98, 103; *Bd.* 60. 18: outemu gehleoðre *stefne* sungon; 314. 21: Endebyrdnesse and ðeaw ðæs songes ewicre stæfne (L. viva voce) sangeras lærde; *Æ. LS.* 7. 44: His mædenu me singað mid geswegum *stemnum*; *Æ. H.* 2. 352. 15; *Hy.* 7. 11: aure *stefne*; 9. 36; *R.* 9. 5: Eald æfensceop eorlum bringe blisse in burgum, ðonne ic bugendre *stefne* styrme; *El.* 747—749: singað in wuldre hædrum *stefnum* heofoncininges lof, woða wlitegaste and ðas word civeðað clænum *stefnum*; *Ph.* 135: we hearpan blyn ne hæleða *stefn* ænges on corðan, ne ænig ðara dreama, ðe dryhten gesceop gumum to gliwe; *An.* 873: heredon on hehðohalgan *stefne*; *Gifts of Men* 94: hafað healice beorhte *stefne.*

II. Figurative use of the word.
Bd. 266. 26: gif ðu songes *stefne* gehyrde; *Chr.* 1062: sio byman stefen; *Sat.* 172: ðære byrhtestan beman *stefne*, 238: wuldres sweg, beman *stefne*; *Dan.* 179; *Ph.* 497.

Stemn, see **Stefn.**

Stocc: a trumpet.
Lind. Mt. 6. 2: Mið ðy ðonne ðu doas ælmessa nelle ðu bema ł *stocc* (L. tuba) singa before ðee.

Streng: a string of a musical instrument.
Æ. Gl. 302. 3: *streng*: fidis; *W. W.* 239. 1: *strengum*: fidibus i. fidis cithare; 406. 19: *strengum*: fidibus; 512. 11: *strengum*: fidibus; *Hpt. Gl.* 520. 2: mid riscendum *strengum*: argutis fidibus.
Lchdm. 3. 262. 14: Cimbalan oððe psalteras oððe *strengas* ætriuan saca hit [getacnað]; *G. PC.* 175. 6: Hwæt cueðe we ðonne hwelce sin ða iungeðoneas mon[n]a buton suelce sumere hearpan *strengas* aðenede, ða se hearpere suiðe ungelice tiehð and styreð, and mid ðy gedeð ðæt hi nawuht ungelice ðæm sone ne singað ðe he wilnað.

In translation from the Scriptures.
Chorda: *V. Ps.* 32. 2; 143. 9; 150. 4; *C. Ps.* 32. 2; 91, 4; *Spl. Ps.* 32. 2; 91. 3; 150. 4; *Th. Ps.* 32. 2; 91. 3; 143. 10; *Blick. Gl.* 32. 2; *Th. Ps.* 67. 21: tympanis togenum *strengum* (without L. equivalent).

Stund: a signal made with a bell, or perhaps, by metonymy, the bell itself (L. signum).

DCM. 215: Geendedum soðlice ðrim gebednm fram cildrum si sweged oðer taen ł *stund* sittendum callum on setlum hyra, 219: ongemang soðlice geenyllendum oðrum *stundum* and geeudednm mid ðam sylfum sealmum hi onginnan ðone uht sang, 592: Syððan on ðam fæce ðe *stunda* beon gehringede gan ða ðewas on fon snædinege.

Sueglhorn, see Sweglhorn.

Suinsung, see Swinsung.

Sunnanūhta: Sunday matins, see PMLA.

Swēg: 1. melodious sound. 2. musical instruments (by metonymy).

W. W. 205. 26: *swegas*: classica; 228. 40: mid gedremum *swege*: eque sonore; 374. 26: *swege*: classica; 527. 19: *swege*: classica; 531. 35: *sweg*: classica.

I. Melodious sound.

A. Of heavenly singing.

Gu. 1269: Engla ðreatas sigeleoð sungon; *sweg* wæs on lyfte gehyred under heofonum, haligra dream, 1296; *Ph.* 618: Swinsað sibgedryht *swega* mæste hædre ymb ðæt halge heahseld godes; *Shrn.* 74. 4: Da com *sweg* suðaneastan of ðære lyfte swa swa micelra fugla *sweg* and gesetton on ðæt hus ðær he inne wæs.

B. Of the singing of mortals.

Herr. Arch. 45: twa cild mid gedremum *swege* singan hludre stefne 'Kyrielejson', 87, 105: Nihtsang sy eae mid gedremum *swege* (L. aeque sonore) gesungen; (?) *Gr. Pr.* 3. 3. 481.

C. Of the singing of birds.

Ph. 131: Bið ðæs hleoðres *sweg* eallum songeræftum swetra and wlitigra and wynsumra wrenea gehwyleum; *Seaf.* 21: ganetes hleoðor and huilpan *sweg*.

D. Of musical instruments.

1. The harp.

Gen. 1081: Dara anum wæs Jabal noma, se ðurh gleawne gedane herbuendra hearpan ærest handum sinum hlyn awehte, swinsigende *sweg* sunu Lameches; *B.* 89; *Bl.* 168. 1; *Za. Ap.* 27. 13: Heo mid winsumum sange gemægnde ðare hearpan *sweg*, 29.

2. The bell.

Shrn. 149. 9: Heo gehyrde bellan *sweg*; *Æ. H.* 156. 6.

II. In translation from the Scriptures.

Symphonia: *Skt. Lk.* 15. 25.—Organum: *C. Ps.* 136. 2.—Tympanum: *C. Ps.* 80. 3; 149. 3.—Sonus (tubae): *C. Ps.* 150. 3; *V. Ps.* 150. 3; *Spl. Ps.* 150. 3.—Clangor (tubae): *Ex.* 19. 16.—Sonitus (tubae): *Ex.* 19. 19; 20. 18.

Swēgan: to sound melodiously, [to sound].
Hpt. Gl. 445. 21: swegde: increpuerit (musica).

I. Applied to singing.
ASH. 2. 14: Þe stefn gedryme *swege* (concrepet); 7. 25: Þe ure stefn ærest *swege* (sonet); 115. 15: Wuldor fæder gedrymum uton *swegan* (personemus) mid stefnum; *Æ. H.* 2. 202. 23.

II. Applied to the sounding of a bell.
DCM. 215: si *sweged* (sonetur) oðer tacn, 380, 953, oð ðæt ðæt forme tacn undernes *swege* (sonuerit).

Swēgcræft: the art of music.
Zu. Ap. 27. 13—18: Þa ongunnon ealle ða men hi herian on hyre *swegcræft*, and Apollonius ana swigode. Þa cwæð se cyninge: 'Apolloni, nu ðu dest yfele, forðam ðe calle men heriað mine dohtor on hyre *swegcræfte*, and ðu ana hi swigende tælst'. Apollonius cwæð: 'eala ðu goda cynge, ic secge ðæt ðin dohtor gefeol on *swegcræft*, ac heo næfð hine na wel geleornod'.

Swēge: harmonious, concordant.
W. W. 129. 39: sum *swege* sang: canticum.

Swegelhorn, see Sweglhorn.

?Swēghlēoðor: musical sound, [sound, noise, clamor].
Ph. 137: Bið ðæs hleoðres sweg eallum songcræftum swetra and wlitigra and wynsumra wrenca gehwylcum. Ne magon ðam breahtme byman ne hornas, ne hearpan hlyn ne hæleða stefn ænges on eorðan ne organan, *swegleoðres* geswin ne swanes feðre, ne ænig ðara dreama, ðe dryhten gescop gumum to gliwe in ðas geomran woruld; *Pa.* 42: *Sweghleoðor* cymeð, woða wynsumast ðurh ðæs wildres muð.

Sweglhorn: a musical instrument, probably stringed.
W. W. 44. 37: *sueglhorn*: sambucus; *Hpt. Gl.* 445. 21: *swegelhorna*: sambucorum (gl. simphoniarum, i. cithararum); *Corpus Gl.* 1777: *sueglhorn*: sambucus.

Swēglīc: sonorous.
DCM. 675: on æfen eallswa mid *sweglicre* stefne (L. sonora voce).

Sweglrād: music, modulation (?).
Rim. P. 29: Scyl wæs hearpe hlude hlynede hleoðor dynede *sweglrad* swinsade.

Swētswēge: sweet-sounding.
   ASH. 58. 16: mid *swetswegum* leoðum (L. suavisonis carminibus).
Swinn: melody.
   Hpt. Gl. 467. 5: *swinne* ł sangge: melodia (gl. cantilena, laude);
   515. 10: *swinn*: melodiam.
Swinsang: melody.
   W. W. 446. 29: *swinsang*: melodia, see Sievers' 'Zu den Ags.
   Glossen', Anglia 13. p. 330: '*W. W.* 446. 29: melodia: swinsang;
   lies swinsung'.
Swinsian: to make melodious sound, to sing.
   R. S. 7: Frætwe mine swogað hlude and *swinsiað* torhte singað;
   Scop. 105: Illude bi hearpan hleoðor *swinsade*; (?) *El.* 240: Bord oft
   onfeng ofer earhgeblond yða swengas, sæ *swinsade*; *Ph.* 124, 140:
   Singeð swa and *swinsað* sælum geblissad, 618: *Swinsað* sibgedryht
   swega mæste hædre ymb ðæt halge heahseld godes; *B.* 611: Dær wæs
   hæleða hleahtor, hlyn *swynsode*, word wærun wynsume; (?) *Chr.* 885;
   Rim. P. 29; *Gen.* 1081: Se ðurh gleawne geðanc herbnendra hearpan
   ærest handum sinum hlyn awehte, *swinsigende* sweg sunu Lamehes;
   Th. Ps. 143. 10.
Swinsung: melody, harmony, air.
   W. W. 342. 39: dream, *swinsunge*: armonia; 446. 28: *swinsunga*:
   melos; 520. 13: *swinsunge*: armonia; *Hpt. Gl.* 438. 18: wynsumne
   swinsunge: melodiam; 467. 21: mid gedremere *swinsunge*: consona
   vocis harmonia; 498. 8: *swinsung*: harmonia; 519. 17: gedremere
   swinsunge: consona melodia (gl. i. cantu); *Corpus Gl.* 195: *swin-
   sung*: armonia.
   Bd. 344. 26.
Swinsungcræft: music.
   W. W. 442. 12: *swinsungcræft*: musicam.
Swīðswēge: melodious, [strong, heroic].
   Hpt. Gl. 416. 1: mid *swiðswium* (= swiðswegum?) sangum dreames:
   dulcisonis (gl. jocundis) melodiae (gl. praeconio).
Tācen: a signal made with a bell, or perhaps, by metonymy,
   the bell itself (L. signum). [a signal, indication].
   A. Used to announce the canonical hours or the various
   observances of the monastic day. (Some of the follow-
   ing passages may refer to the signal given by the
   hand.)
   DCM. 246: Ongynnan primsang buton bellan *tacne*, 247, 272:
   Cildran soðlice cyrcean ingangendum cyrewerd ærest hringe *tan*
   (n. *tacn*), 376: oð ðæt hi eft gesealdum *tacne* non don, 382, 475,
   506: Eallum *tacnum* gestiredum sigedon mæsse, æfter ðam lofu
   dægrædlice, 954, 957; *BR.* 75. 15.

B. Used in the services.

DCM. 215: geendedum soðlice ðrim gebedum fram cildrnm si sweged oðer *tacn* ł stund sittendum eallum on setlum hyra.

Tēnstrenge: ten-stringed, (L. decacordus).
    V. Ps. 91. 4: *tenstrenge* hearpan; *Spl. Ps.* 91. 3: *tynstrengum*; 143. 11.

Tēnstrenged: ten-stringed, (L. decacordus).
    Blick. Gl. tynstrengedum: decacordo.
    Lamb. Ps. 91. 4: *tynstrængedum*; 143. 9: *tynstrængdom*.

Tīdsang: the hour services, canonical hours, see *PMLA*.

Timpana: a drum, timbrel. 2. a timpan, see Introduction.
    G. PC. 347. 4: 'Lofiað God mid *tympanan* and on choro'. Se *tympano* bið geworht of drygum felle, and ðæt fell hlyt, ðonne hit mon sliehð.

In translation from the Scriptures.
    Tympanum: *V. Ps.* 67. 26; 80. 3; 149. 3; 150. 4; *C. Ps.* 67. 26; *Th. Ps.* 67 24; 149. 3; *Genesis* 31. 27.

Timpestere: a (female [?]) timbrel-player.
    Lamb. Ps. 67. 26: *timpestera*: tympanistriarum.

Traht: a slow sad anthem sung without response (L. tractus).
    DCM. 743: fyliað *traht* [eripe me domine], §55.

Tropere: a book containing the tropes used in the High Mass (L. troparium).
    CD. 4. 275: And nu ða synd .ii. fulle sangbec and .i. nihtsang and .i. *tropere* and .ii. salteras; *Techmer* 2. 119. 11: Ðonne ðu *tropere* haban wille, ðonne wege ðu ðine swiran hand and tyrn mid ðinum swiðran scytefingre ofer ðine breost foreweard swilce ðu notian wille.

Truð: a trumpet-player, [buffoon].
    Æ. Gr. 40. 7: *truð*: liticen; *Æ. Gl.* 302. 8: *truð*: liticen.
    Æ. LS. 12. 59: On ðære ylcan wucan com sum *truð* to ðæs bisceopes hirede, se ne gymde nanes lenctenes fæstnes ac eode him to kicenan, ða hwile ðe se bisceop mæssode and began to etenne.

Truðhorn: a trumpet.
    Æ. Gl. 302. 8: *truðhorn* oððe sarga: lituus; *Hpt. Gl.* 423. 9: *truðhornes*: salpistae (the passage is: horrorem belli et classicae salpistae metuentes).

Tunnebotm: a barrel-head used for a drum.
    W. W. 123. 10: *tunnebotm*: tympanum.

Tympana, see Timpana.

Tȳnstrenge, see Tēnstrenge.

Tȳnstrænged, -strenged, see Tēnstrenged.

?Drēat: a choral dance, [crowd, host, band].
 In translation from the Scriptures.
  Chorus: *V. Ps.* 149. 3; 150. 4; *C. Ps.* 149. 3; 150. 4; *Th. Ps.* 149. 3.
?Drymm: a choral band, [crowd, noise, glory].
  Chr. 388: a bremende unaðreotendum *drymmum* singað.
Ūhtsang: matins, see *PMLA*.
Ūhtsanglīc: nocturnal, see *PMLA*.
Undernsang: tierce, see *PMLA*.
Undersingan: to accompany a song.
  Æ. Gr. 151. 2: ic *undersinge* oððe orgnige: occino.
Ungedrȳme: discordant, inharmonious.
  Hall.
Ungeswēge: discordant, inharmonious, [dissonant].
  W. W. 129. 38: *ungeswege* sang: diaphonia.
Welgestemned: having a good voice.
  Herr. Arch. 45: twa cild *welgestemnede* mid gedremum swege singan hindre stefne 'Kyrielejson'.
(?) Weorðian: to praise in song, (L. psallere).
  Th. Ps. 134. 3: weorðiað his naman.
Wered, see Werod.
Werod: a choral dance.
 In translation from the Scriptures and hymns.
  Chorus: *Spl. Ps.* 149. 3; 150. 4; *Th. L.* 15. 15; *ASH.* 51. 7; 55. 11; 57. 6; 111. 21; 137. 29.
?Wīglēoð: a battle song? war cry?
  Exod. 221: Gemundon weardas *wigleoð*.
Wistle, see Hwistle.
Wōplēoð: a funeral song or dirge.
  Hpt. Gl. 488. 3: *wopleoð* ł birisang ł liesang: tragoediam, (gl. miseriam, luctum).
?Wordgidd: a lay, elegy.
  B. 3173: Ða ymbe hlæw riodan hildediore, æðelinga bearn ealra twelfa, woldon ceare cwiðan, kyning mænan, *wordgyd* wrecan and ymb wer sprecan.
Wordgyd, see Wordgidd.
?Wōð: melodious vocal sound, [speech, sound, cry].
  R. 9. 11: hæleðum bodige wilcumena fela *woðe* minre; *El.* 749: Singallice singað in wuldre hædrum stefnum heofoncininges lof, *woða* wlitegaste and ðas word cweðað clænum stefnum; *Pa.* 42: Sweghleoðor cymeð, *woða* wynsumast ðurh ðæs wildres muð.

? **Wōðcræft:** 1. song. 2. [the art of poetry].
I. Song.
    Ph. 127: Wrixleð *woðcræfte* wundorlicor beorhtan reorde, ðonne æfer byre monnes hyrde under heofonum.
II. [The art of poetry].
    Whale 2: Ic wille woðcræfte wordum cyðan bi ðam hwale; *Ph.* 548.

? **Wōðgiefu:** the gift of song.
    R. 32. 18: hwæðre hyre is on fote fæger hleoðor, wynlicu *woðgiefu.*

[**Wōðsang**]: a song, (poem).
    Chr. 46: witgena *woðsong.*

Woðsong, see Woðsang.

? **Wrecan:** to sing, [utter, recite].
    Wond. Cre. 12: ðæt geara in gliwes cræfte mid gieddingum guman oft *wrecan*; *B.* 1065: Þær wæs sang and sweg samod ætgædere, gomenwudu greted, gid oft *wrecen,* ðonne healgamen Hroðgares scop æfter medobence mænan scolde; *An.* 1549.

? **Wrenc:** melody, [modulation of the voice].
    Ph. 133: Bið ðæs hleoðres sweg eallum songcræftum swetra and wynsumra *wrenca* gehwylcum.

Wynpsalterium: a joyous psaltery, (L. psalterium).
    Th. Ps. 56. 10: Aris, *wynpsalterium.*

Ymen: 1. a hymn. 2. a sacred song. (L. hymnus.)
I. Hymn of the church.
    BR. 51. 1; *Gr. BR.* 33. 12: Æfter ðysum is *ymen* to singenne, ðe to ðære tide belimpð; 36. 21; 38. 11; 40. 23; 41. 5, 11; 41. 23; 43. 2; 44. 3; *DCM.* 445, 446, 452—454: Swiðe mærum soðlice and freolsicum symel tidum *ymnas* gelimplice gewunan gesungenne gewunelicum to cymes soðlice drihten lenctenes and ðrowunge timan *ymnas* ðæs sylfan begeneges rihtlice beon gesungene swa ðeah hwæðere ðæt na ða *ymnas* be ðam fæstene ac ða ðe ðurh eall gear yrnað sunnan dagum oððe nihtum timan lenctenlicum beon gesungene, 901, 1027; *BH.* 147. 3; 151. 9; *St. Gu.* 18. 13; *Vesp. H.* 12. 6; 13. 22.

II. A sacred song.
  A. [A poem].
    Smith's Bd. 587. 16: be ðam *hymene* ðe we be hire geworhton.
  B. In translation from the Scriptures.
    Hymnus: *V. Ps.* 39. 4; 64. 2, 14; 99. 4; 118. 171; 136. 3; *C. Ps.* 39. 4; 64. 2, 14; 99. 4; 118. 171; 136. 3; *Spl. Ps.* 99. 4; 136. 4; *Th. Ps.* 118. 171; 136. 4; *Rush. M.* 26. 30; *Lind. M.* 26. 30.

Ymenboc: a book of hymns (L. librum hymnorum).
Bd. 484. 23: *ymenbec* missenlice metre.

Ymener: a book of hymns.
CD. 4. 275: Nu ða synd .ii. salteras and .ii. *ymneras*; *Cart. Sax.*
3. 660. 32: Þær synd twa Cristes bec, and .i. mæsseboc, and .i. *ymener*, and .i. salter; *Techmer* 2. 121. 9: *Hymneres tacen is ðæt mon wæege bradlinga his hand and rære up his litlan finger.*

Ymensang: a hymn.
Gr. Dial. 2, 3, 4.

Appendixes.

I.
Latin and Old English Equivalents.

agere: singan.
antiphon: antefn.
antiphonarium: antefnere.
ars musica: glīgcræft.
aule: bȳmere.
auledus: rēodpīpere.
avena: hwistle.
barbita: bīeme.
Benedicite: blētsingsealm.
bicinium: twegra sang.
buccina: bīeme, horn.
buccinare: bȳmian, blȳrian.
camena: sangpīpe.
campana: belle, clugge, motbell.
canere: galan, herian, singan.
cautabilis: singendlic.
cantare: cwēman, gesingan, singan.
cantatio: sang.
— leta: lewisplega.
cantator ecclesiae: ciricsangere.
canticum: cantic, cwide, lofsang, psalm æfter hærpsansang, sang, sōn, sum swēge sang.
— laetitiae: blissesang.
cantilena: fitt, sangdrēam.
cantio: drēamness, galdor, sang.
cantor: cantere, cantor, sangere.
cantrix: sangestre.
cantus: sang.

carmen: fitt, galdorlēoð, lēoð, lofsang.
— ad mensam: bēodfers.
— ecclesiasticum: ciricsang.
— funebre: līclēoð.
celebrare: singan.
celeuma: lewisplega.
ceminigi: hearpanstala.
cereaeus: hornblāwere.
cereuma: lewisplega.
cerimingius: hearpanstapas.
chorda: streng.
chorea: hlūddra sang.
chorus: chōr, chōrglēo, lofsang, sang, ðrēat, werod.
cithara: cytere, hearpslege, hearpswēg, hearpung.
citharista: hearpestre, hearpere.
citharizare: hearpian.
citharoedus: hearpere.
clangere: blāwan.
clangor: swēg.
classica: bīeme, swēg.
classicum: blædhorn.
clocca: belle.
cloccarium: bellhūs.
collectaneum: collectaneum.
concentus: drēam, efenhlēoðru g, sang.

concentor: midsingend.
concha: bīeme.
concinere: hlēoðrian.
concrepare: hlēoðrian, swēgan.
consonus: gedrēme, gehlēoð.
cornea: horn.
cornicen: hornblāwere.
cornu: horn, fyhtehorn.
crepitaculum: cleadur.
cymbalum: belle, cimbal.
decacordus: tēnstrenge, tēnstrenged.
decantare: singan, āsingan.
decantatio: sang.
diaphonia: ungeswēge sang.
dicere: singan.
dulcisonis: swīðswēge.
epicediou: līcsang.
epithalamium: brýdlēoð, brýdsang, giftlēoð.
fausta adclamantes: lofsang.
fidicen: fiðelere, glīgmann, hearpere.
fidicina: fiðelestre.
fidicula: fiðele.
fidis: streng.
fistula: hwistle.
flare: blāwan.
gradual: graðul.
harmonia: drēam, geðwǣre sang, swinsung.
hymeneus: brýdsang.
hymnizantes: lofsingende.
hymnus: bēodfers, lofsang, ymen.
incantare: galan, singan.
incantatio: galdor.
increpare: swēgan.
insonare: blāwan.
jubilare: drēmau, singan.
jubilatio: drēam, sang.
laus: lofsang.
letania: letania.
liber hymnorum: ymenboc.
liticen: truð.
lituus: sārga.
magister ecclesiasticae cautionis: magister sanges.
melodia: drēam, sealmsang, swinn, swinsang, swinsung.
modulari: singan.

modulus: drēam.
musa: pipe, hwistle.
musica: drēamcræft, glīg, mirigness, sangcræft, söncræft, swinsungcræft.
musicus: drēamere, drēamlīc, gliwhlēoðriendlīc, pīplīc.
occinere: singan.
offertorium: lānesang, offerenda.
organum: drēam, swēg, organa, orgeldrēam, orgenadrēam.
peragere: singan.
personare: swēgan.
plectrum: hearpenægl, hearpslege, nægl, sceacel, scearu, slegel.
precentor: foresingend, heahsangere.
psallere: āsingan, drēman, asingan, herian, salletan, sealmlof ewēðan, sealmlofian, sealm singan, singan, weorðian.
psalmodia: drēam, sealmsang.
psalmus: ær hearpansang, hearpsang, lof, sealm, sealmlof.
psalterium: hearpe, psalterium, sælterium, saltere, sealmglīg, sealmlēoð, sealmlof, sealmsang, wynpsalterium.
pulsare: cnyllan, hringan.
recitare: singan.
resonare: singan.
respondere: andswarian.
responsorium: reps.
salpica: bymesangere.
salpinx: bīeme, sārga.
salpista: býmere, truðhorn.
salpix: horn.
sambucus: sweglhorn.
signum: bēacen, cnyll, stund, tācen.
sonare: swēgan.
sonitus: swēg.
sonor: swēg.
sonorus: geswēge, swēglīc.
sonus: drēam, hlēoðor, sōn, swēg.
suavisonus: swētswēge.
succentor: æftersingend.
succinere: orgnian, undersingan.
symphonia: answēgesang, hwistlung, swēg.

temelici (Θυμελικός): Idel sangere.
thessera: bīeme.
tibia: hwistle.
tibicen: pīpere, hwistlere.
tintinnabulum: belle, cimbal.
tractus: traht.
tragoedia: sārliclēoð, wōplēoð.
trenos: sārlīc sang.
troparium: tropere.
tuba: bīeme, horn, stocc.
— classica: bīeme, scypbȳme.

tubicen: bȳmere, glīgmann, hwistlere.
tympanista: glīgmann.
tympanistria: glīewmēden, timpestere.
tympanum: glīgbēam, hearpe, hylsong, swēg, timpana.
vas: fæt.
vasum psalmi: scalmfæt.
versus: fers.
vox: stefn.

II.
Modern English and Old English Equivalents.

anthem: antefn.
  offertory —: lānesang, offerenda, offringsang.
  slow, sad —: traht.
antiphonary: antefnere.
bagpipe: pīpe, sangpīpe.
bell: belle, bēacen, cimbal, clugge, tācen.
church —: ciricbelle.
  — clapper: clipol, clipur.
  hand —: handbelle.
  — house: bellhūs.
  moot —: mōtbell.
  to ring —: cnyllan, hringan.
  — ringing: belhring.
  signal made with —: bēacen, belltācen, stund, tācen.
  sound of —: cnyll.
bewail: besingan.
canonical service: tīdsang.
  compline: nihtsang.
  lauds: lofsang.
  mass celebration: mæssesang.
  matins: æftersang, dægrēdsang, lofsang, ūhtsang.
  none: nōnsang.
  prime: prīmsang.
  sext: middægsang.

tierce: undernsang.
  vespers: æfensang.
canticle: cantic, lofsang, organ.
chant: sōn.
choir: chōr.
choral—band: ðrymm.
  — dance: chōr, chòrglēo, ðrēat, werod.
chorus: drēam.
cithara: cȳtere.
collect: collectaneum.
crwth: crwth.
cymbal: cimbal.
cymbalum: cimbal, belle.
drum: timpana, tunnebotm.
enchant: begalan, besingan, galan.
fiddle: fiðele.
  player on —: fiðelere.
  female player on —: fiðelestre.
gradual: graðul.
glee: glīg.
  — maiden: gīlewmēden.
harmonious: ānswēge, gedrēme, gehlēoð, geswēge, geðwǣre, swēge.
harmony: drēam, efenhlēoðor, efenhlēoðrung, swinsung.
harp: glīgbēam, gomenwudu, hearpe.
  art of playing —: swēgcræft.

neck of —: hearpanstala, hearpanstapas.
to play —: grētan, hearpian.
player of —: hearpere.
female player of —: hearpestre.
— playing: gearobrygd, hearpslege, hearpung.
sound of —: hearpswēg.
— string: hearpestreng, suēr, streng.
horn: horn.
battle —: fyhtchorn.
— bearer: hornbora.
to blow —: āðēotan.
— blower: hornbläwere.
forest —: blēðhorn.
war —: güðhorn.
hymn: lof, lofsang, sang, ymen, ymensang.
— book: sangbōc, ymenbōc, ymener.
— singing: lofsingende.
— sung at meal time: bēodfers.
inharmonious: ungedrȳme, ungeswēge.
lay: gidd, lēoð, wordgidd, gidding.
death —: füslēoð.
evening —: æfenlēoð.
horrible —: gryrelēoð.
minstrel's —: ewidegidd.
noble —: dryhtlēoð.
sad —: gēomorgid.
sorrowful: sorhlēoð.
war —: güðlēoð, hildelcoð.
litany: letania.
minstrel: gligmann, glīwhlēoðriend.
ale-house —: ealuscōp.
art of —: gligcræft.
evening —: æfensceop.
melodious: drēme, gedrēme, swiðswēge.
— sound: swēg, wöð.
melody: drēam, drēamswinsung, geswin(s), gliwstæf, hlēoðor, mirigness, swinn, swinsang, swinsung, wrenc (?).
modulated: gedrēmed.
modulation: sweglrād.
music: beorhtm, drēam, hlēoðor,

hlyn(n), hwistlung, sangcræft, sangdrēam, sōn, sōncræft, swegelrād, swinsungcræft.
art of —: drēamcræft.
ecclesiastical —: ciricsang.
glee —: glīg.
to make —: dreman.
musical: drēamlic, gliwhlēoðriendlic, piplic.
— instrument: drēam, organa, orgeldrēam, orgenadrēam, swēg, swēglhorn.
to play —: getēon, glēowian, plegean.
to string —: glēowian.
— sound: swēghlēoðor, hlyn(n).
musician: drēamere.
organ: organa.
pipe: hwistle, pīpe.
— music: pipdrēam.
— player: hwistlere, pīpere, rēodpīpere, sangpīpe.
plectrum: hearpenægl, hearpslege, nægl, seeacel, seearn, slegel.
praise in song: weorðian.
prayer: gebed.
psalm(s): hearpsang, lofsang, sang, scalm, scalmsang.
— 148: lofscalm.
book of —: saltere, scalmbōc, scalmsang.
— praise: scalmlof.
selection of —: saltere, scalmgetæl, scalmlēoð.
— singing: scalmsang.
— utterance: scalmcwide.
psalmist: scalmscop, scalmwyrhta.
psalter: saltere, scalmsang.
psaltery: psalterium, sælterium, saltere.
joyous —: wynpsalterium.
rattle: cleadur.
resonant: scyll.
respond antiphonally: andswarian.
response: reps.
sing: āsingan, āwrecan, galan, gesingan, giddian, leoðian, singan, swinsian, wrecan.

sing — voice.

— mass: mæssian.
— melodiously: hleoðrian.
— over a person: ofersingan.
— portentous music: āgalan.
— praises: herian.
— sacred music: sealmian, sealmlofian.
singable: singendlic.
singer: sangere.
assistant —: midsingend.
evening —: æfenscēop.
female —: sangestre.
leader of church music: cantere, cantor, ciricsangere, foresingend, hēahsaugere.
responsive —: æftersingend.
teacher of ecclesiastical music: magister sanges.
singing: dreamness.
to serve by —: cweman.
song: cwide, drȳme, fitt, hleoðorcwide, gidd, lēoð, leoðgidding, lēoðsang, organ, sang, wōðcræft, wōðsang.
art of —: sangercræft, woðcræft.
— of enchantment: ceargealdor, galdor, galdorlēoð.
funeral —: bergelsang, birisang, byrgensang, liclēoð, licsang, sarliclēoð, wōplēoð.
gift of —: wōðgiefu.
gleeman's —: gidd, glēoword, scēawendwīse.
— of grief: hearmlēoð.
— to the harp: hearpsang.

— of joy: blissesong.
marriage —: brȳdlēoð, brȳdsang, giftlēoð.
— of praise: lof, lofsang.
rowing —: lewisplega, sǣlēoð.
sacred —: cantic, sealm, ymen.
skilled in —: lēoðcræftig.
— of triumph: sigelēoð.
war —: fyrdlēoð, wīglēoð.
sonorous: swēglic.
sound — melodiously: nēomian, swegan, swinsian.
— shrilly: scralletan.
sweet-sounding: swētswēge.
ten-stringed: tēnstrenge(d).
timbrel: hylsong, timpanum.
— player: timpestere.
timpan: timpana.
tone: sōn.
troper: tropere.
trumpet: bleme, blǣdhorn, sarga, stocc, swēg, trūðhorn.
to blow —: āblāwan, blāwan, bȳmian, galan, hlȳrian.
blowing of —: blāwung.
heavenly —: heofonbȳme.
ship —: scypbȳme.
sound of —: drēam.
war —: horobȳme.
trumpeter: bȳmere, bȳmesaugere, hornblāwere, hornbora, truð.
verse: fers.
voice: stefn.
having a good —: welgestemned.

Corrections in the Glossary.

Beorhtm, *Clipol*, *Dreamswinsung*, and *Gedrēmed* are to be inclosed in brackets, and the mark of interrogation is to be removed from *Dreamswinsung*.—The reference *Somner* is to be added under *Crud*.—Under *Gedrēmed* add: *Prud. Gl.* 390. 35: *gedrym yd*: modulata.—In the eleventh line under *Cantic* read *exultavit* and *audivi*.

www.ingramcontent.com/pod-product-compliance
Lightning Source LLC
Chambersburg PA
CBHW020125170426
43199CB00009B/641